Discourses and Essays

Discourses and Essays

BY
COUNT FRANCIS BICKERSTAFFE-DREW
(JOHN AYSCOUGH, pseud.)

Essay Index Reprint Series

originally published by

B. HERDER BOOK CO.

BOOKS FOR LIBRARIES PRESS
FREEPORT, NEW YORK

First Published 1922
Reprinted 1970

NIHIL OBSTAT

Ludovici, die 13. Julii, 1922.
F. G. Holweck,
Censor Librorum

IMPRIMATUR

Sti. Ludovici, die 17. Julii, 1922.
✠*Joannes J. Glennon,*
Archiepiscopus
Sti. Ludovici

STANDARD BOOK NUMBER:
8369-1489-9

LIBRARY OF CONGRESS CATALOG CARD NUMBER:
78-107683

PRINTED IN THE UNITED STATES OF AMERICA

This little book is dedicated

to

THE VERY REV. JOHN CAVANAUGH, D.D.,

of the

Society of the Holy Cross

CONTENTS

CONTENTS

THE CHURCH AND VANITY FAIR

ELSEWHERE we have spoken of the charge
brought against the Church, not by her
more reputable opponents, of her inferior
morality. We venture to believe that no single human being who ever considered her claims, with the
faintest genuine intention of submitting to her,
should he find those claims to rest on justice and
right reason, has ever been decided against submission by a frank conviction that in becoming a Catholic he would be accepting a lower rule of ethics.

No student of her history and of that of the
world, we are firmly convinced, has ever failed to
arrive at the conclusion that her stand has consistently been on the side of good. Her vicissitudes
have been great, her trials very many; and they
would have been much less had she held the easy
principles, the convenient laxity, the accommodating
readiness to sacrifice justice for temporal, or selfish,
advantage with which the ignorant and the vulgar-witted have credited her.

In history she is seen, time and again, at variance
with the mighty. She might have lived more
pleasantly at ease had she been willing to snatch at
suggested compromises, to barter unchanging rules
of right for comfortable expedients; to condone

1

robberies and take a present for herself; to wink at evil in high places and abstain from visiting upon the powerful the same censures into which the meanest of her children would have fallen who had attempted similar infractions of the law of God. It is not because she has been lax that she has stirred up against herself potent adversaries, at one period or another, in every country of Christendom, but precisely because she would hold no treaty with laxity though the favour of emperors or kings might have been the reward of her compliance.

Of all this the candid and not lazy student becomes fully aware. The libellers of the Church's moral rectitude are not the learned, and the sincere, nor the clearminded, but the shallow and ignorant, the malignant, and they who invert the quality of charity that thinketh no evil and rejoiceth not in iniquity. There is no more practical proof of fondness for anything than being willing to pay for it, and it is to hear of iniquity that they pay who go rejoicingly to the regale on the "experiences" of escaped monks and escaped nuns.

But that word of charity reminds inevitably of a special difference between the Church's attitude towards evil and that of the un-Catholic world. Towards unrepentant sin the Church holds herself rigidly: till the evil thing be put away she shuts up her treasures, and lifts an ever-threatening hand of warning. No sacrament of hers can avail the impenitent; no reconciliation can be held with him. No lapse of time can purge his fault while to that fault he cleaves lovingly or obstinately, nor death itself if death shall have brought no penitence. She does not judge the dead; vengeance is not her's but God's; but neither does she presume to pronounce sentence of acquittal simply because death has intervened; death may have been, for all she can see, but the final hopeless seal on a life-long evil compact. Him who has died under every outward presumption of impenitence she does not declare absolved by death; he has passed beyond her jurisdiction and, in awe, to God's Omniscience she leaves him.

But if he arise from the foul meal of swinish husks, and from the alien land where he has dwelt in folly, turn his eyes homeward, wistfully, then does she run to meet him. Afar off she yearns to him, and midway she encounters him with kindest embracing; and, at his word of penitence, the golden chain of love is for his neck, the clean garment of reconciliation is for his sin-worn frame. She calls him to his father's table, and of all his wanton past there is no chatter heard, she makes no gibe and will hear none; if an elder son would cavil at her kindness she stills him with a gentle reproof: "Son, thou hast been always with me. This my brother, was lost and is found," His wicked past is dead; let the dead bury their dead. She bids him look forward; after the first sorrowful tears for the deeds of exile are shed he is to bring forth fruit meet for repentance, and must make haste to sow for a better harvest, and to that end labour; it is not she that will hold him with hopeless face pressed down into the old mire, nor she that dubs him Prodigal returned, but the common, harsh label.

And this is what the un-Catholic world, that goes sinning smugly on, cannot away with. It is not hard on unrepentant sin. It knows of it, and nudges a little and smiles a good deal, and winks humanly, and is not very angry nor greatly scandalised. It has a kindness for wild oats, and does not perceive them to be much out of season, though planted by quite elderly sowers. It dines with the sower and drinks his wine, and avails itself of the pleasant crumbs of his wealth, though he be sowing still after fifty seasons—or she, for that matter. He is a good fellow, or she is a "good sort." That he, or she, may be outraging God is nothing to it; God is nothing to it either. The most elderly wild-oats need be no offence against society. There be gentlemanly oats, and lady-like, though stale and stinking, foul and fetid, rotten and rot-breeding; oats that help the prostitute to hell and drag the well-bred, well-washed adulteress thither, but conventional, look you, and, with luck, decently glossed—or at all events indecently. It is all part of the show: a recognised department in Vanity Fair.

It is not to the unrepentant that the jostlers in the Fair are austere, but to the repentant. The repentant have left it, and the tender mercies of the ungodly are no more for them. They are deserters and are to be shot down: their backs are turned, and into them any knife may be thrust. It is when a guilty wretch has ceased to be guilty that Vanity Fair begins to cry out upon him; it is when God has pardoned that the folk in the Fair discover him to be unpardonable. So long as he sticks to the Fair it is mean and unfriendly to note that he *is* misbehaving: when he gives over misbehaving then is it time to proclaim loudly all he has done. What sinless God has forgiven none of these fellows, stuck fast in sin still, will forgive, nor will the women of the Fair. St. Augustine would have been well received in it in his worst days; would he have been received there at all had he shown himself in it when he had been long a saint? Would St. Mary Magdalene? Would any penitent? The repentant sinner may have been leading an exemplary life for years, but every bull in it will gore him, every goat push and butt, every filthy monkey gibber and mouth—because he *is* penitent.

Is this simply hypocrisy in the people of the Fair? They grin at the Church and throw it against her that she will whitewash any scamp who comes to her; do they believe that she will do this for the *unrepentant* sinner? Not they. Nor is the outcry they raise against her simply hypocrisy: it is more. In every reprobate reclaimed by the Church they perceive a loss to the Fair, a captive from their own ranks. That is why they are bitter and scornful against her for doing just what God does. She is the servant, and the servant is not to set herself above her Master, it is enough that she be as her

Master: what He has forgiven she must forgive, what He has cleansed she is not to call unclean still.

We said at the beginning of this paper that no one was ever deterred from becoming a Catholic by an honest conviction that to do so would imply the acceptance of a lower moral standard; but the truth is that many hold back from entering the Church because they plainly recognise that to submit to her would involve the acceptance of a moral standard inconveniently high. To many the idea of joining the Church has never occurred at all: the whole question of religion is tedious to them. To some the idea has occurred, but the cost of following it up is too heavy; it is not merely that there may be, as there often is, some material loss to face: the loss they cannot face is the loss of liberty to lead a life of laxity. They perceive clearly that on Catholics is laid the obligation of a rule of conduct to which they would grudge obedience. Far from believing that the practice of the confessional is an instance of Catholic corruption, a pleasant way of compounding with sin, a comfortable device for enabling folk to live loosely and yet with easy conscience, they are strongly aware that to accept the obligation of the confessional means a definite rupture with the kind of life they are leading, and from which they are unprepared to break off, and that in the confessional is only applied to actual conduct the Church's theoretic rule of ethics.

I believe this to be the real explanation of many half-promised conversions that have never fulfilled themselves. It is not the Church's moral laxity that holds people off, but her moral austerity. Nor was it corruption in religious houses that made the sycophants of Henry VIII glad to see them destroyed; those who had no material profit to make out of their suppression (and we may be sure that many were disappointed of such profit, as many made it) were well pleased to be relieved of the spectacle of the Church's old counsels of perfection in daily practice. And what is true of the sixteenth century is equally true of the eighteenth, the nineteenth, and the twentieth: the wholesale destruction of religious houses is due in part to the desire for spoliation, but in part also to the fact that nothing is more repugnant to those who would destroy both Christ and His law than being compelled to see His law illustrated in its most perfect expression.

Those countries which have most entirely cast off the bit and bridle of the Church rejoice in a freedom of which they are fully aware: the freedom to do what they like. For centuries there has been talk of the intellectual freedom achieved by the Reformation; its real asset, endearing it to millions of wayward human beings, is the moral freedom it suggests. For to the bulk of mankind the absence of law appears freedom; it is only a minority that has ever willingly recognised that in the most perfect law is the most perfect freedom. In England the course of procedure has been this: at first the Reformation cried to the people, "To God only are you answerable: no Pope shall enslave your conscience. From him we emancipate you, and your rule of right shall henceforth be the voice of God alone speaking to your heart." And the ultimate fruit of this axiom of private judgment has been the refusal to teach God to the people, so that they are bred up to know neither Him nor His law, and the voice of conscience is the urging of the personal inclination of each individual.

Can anybody who knows Sweden or Norway, or Holland or Protestant Germany, believe that what the peoples of those countries dread is the intellectual slavery of Catholicism? What they are shy of is the restraint on conduct that was removed by the happy thought of private judgment.

Ask any straightforward young scapegrace and he will confess that there is a delightful unsupernaturalness about the atmosphere of a thoroughly non-Catholic country and society: a cosy absence of any *arrière pensée* of the old bothersome Ten Commandments, a most agreeable sense of being entirely your own master without any other master that matters on earth or above it. And, with equal ingenuousness, he will complain that a thoroughly Catholic society is tiresome to live in; Catholics are not, he admits, "a bad sort"; but the more Catholic they are, the more awkward is it for a fellow who likes to take what's going to be jolly, and not to fuss about the world to come. If a fellow were to be ill, really ill, and rather uncertain of recovery, a typically Catholic household would not, he avows, be a bad place for it—it happened once to himself, and there was a something comfortable about it. But afterwards—

> The devil was ill: the devil a saint would be.
> The devil got well: the devil a saint was he.

When a fellow has *quite* recovered, and the fears of death are gone by, and he is strong enough to be himself again—why, then, the typical Catholic household is not so much the thing. There's too much of the world to come about it, too much no- tion of putting good resolutions in practice: as if religion was not, after all, an accessory of the sick- room, as if it were a matter of common life and five-and-twenty. *That's* where the out-and-out Catholics make their little mistake. The sort of theories everyone has a nodding acquaintance with *as* theories they take *au pièd de la lettre* and carry about with them as a fellow does his ribs—inside but indubitable and of week-a-day significance. He does not wish to imply that they *jaw* a lot, rather the contrary; but they take for granted that admitted principles are things to act on. That's it. Now his own principles are first-rate, but even the best principles can be *de trôp* if you let 'em; the thing is to keep up sides with them, and that's what these thoroughgoing Catholics can't seem to man- age: their principles have them by the nose all the time. Ill or well makes no odds; they aren't, not to say, gloomy even when a fellow is pretty bad and wondering where he'll be to-morrow; no, grave and

awfully kind-hearted, but not solemn, not too d—d
solemn like some are.   Even the priest who looked
in and knew a fellow was a heretic, had a bit of a
joke for him, and told him to buck-up.   Yes, he did;
not a bit in your regulation death-bed manner.
"Buck-up" was the word.   Still they seem to suppose that getting well makes no difference; and
what was true at your worst is true still.

So our candid young scapegrace.

But there are Catholic households which are not
typically Catholic; which our young friend would
readily admit were just like any other households;
where you might easily forget that your enter-
tainers were Catholics at all.   In them there is none
of the supernaturalness so disconcerting in unmistakably Catholic circles.

We do not cite our candid friend as an expert
judge of the supernatural, but merely as an independent witness to certain plain facts concerning
which he is without prejudice.   He belongs not to
us but to the Fair, and his tastes are of it; but he has
a perfect instinct as to what does belong to it, and
he knows accurately what sort of people are in it,
and what are not.   His witness is good so far—
that it is not in typically Catholic circles that a comfortable laxity is to be found, but in circles that are
not Catholic at all, or are so only in name.
Whereas, if the accusation of the Church's enemies
were true, and the Church itself were lax, it would be
precisely among Catholics who most typically rep-
resent her, and most accurately reflect her distinctive

spirit, that laxity of conduct and shallowness of principle would be found.

And this is the conclusion of the whole matter: the Church as she shows herself in a history of nearly two thousand years, has stood immovably for a law that she cannot change nor compromise, because it is not a human specific but a Divine revelation; at no cost of loss or danger to herself can she, or does she, admit modifications of that law, whether in dealing publicly with the States and their rulers, or privately with individuals in the confessional. Where there is transgression of the law she can only admit to reconciliation on repentance and amendment, but where there is repentance she is as ready to forgive as God Himself, and, like Him, will break no bruised reed, will not remember transgression for ever. She will make no demand of fallen man that He does not make. She admits them who *have* been wicked to her table, and is content, as He was, to be fleered at as a friend of publicans and sinners. Where He whispers of hope she will not force those who have been shamed to despair. That pitiless function she leaves to the world, that has as much pity now as it had in Jewry when Christ walked there.

Men, not angels, are her charge, and she remembers we are dust; not with loud yells, vindictive, does she hound the fallen to utter destruction, but out of sinners she fashions saints. The human dust, in her hands, is built up into a man reflecting not the first Adam but the second. And that is her real offence against the world: not that she would make sinners of men, but saints; for it is an undying reproach to the world that saints are possible in it. The existence of saints is an insult to a world that would make Christ's law an allegory or a dream; and the Church, that makes saints out of common, fallen men, is the arch-offender. So they must call her liar and hypocrite—since they would have nothing genuine and sincere but corruption, nothing real but evil. The Church is reviled and miscalled because she affirms God's unchanging law to be always in possession, and will not confess that any modern change can make it obsolete or impracticable. Tender and full of encouragement, as Christ was Himself, to the imperfect, she insists on the possibility of His own counsels of perfection, and will not have them explained away, or ruled out of date. Therein lies the world's grievance against her: if she would indeed teach men that every demand of God can be evaded, every rule of Christian ethic be dispensed, and that Mammon and God can be twin masters, then would the world and Mammon love her well: what an ally she would be! How soon would all the race of man be Satan's, if only the Church would be what her enemies pretend to think she is! If Giant Pope really ruled in Vanity Fair how light-hearted would the folk in the Fair be; how free from chill misgiving—what complaisant, amenable children of his they would all become.

Does any bad Catholic pretend that he is bad

by connivance of the Church? If he be leading a
life immoral, worldly, irreligious, in oblivion of
God's law, selfish, sensual, of mean ideals and hell-
ward purposes, does he whisper to any traducer of
the Church that it is all with her comfortable per-
mission? That such an ecclesiastical custom covers
his case, that such a Pope's decision allows his
licence, or that this or that priest assured him, in the
privacy of the confessional, that he had nothing to
fear? That, so long as he did what Church and
Pope and priest told him, he need not worry about
what God has told us all? Is there any liar bold
enough to pretend that any wretched Catholic has
made this avowal, and that such Catholics are typical of the Church?

That there are bad Catholics we know as well as
we know that, out of the twelve the Master chose
from the whole human race to be His disciples, one
was a devil. But can even they themselves, dearly
as they, and all of us, would love to make false excuse, pretend that their badness is due to the Church,
and not in spite of her? Are they her docile children or her rebels? Was the apostasy of Judas
Christ's fault? Was David called the man after
God's own heart because he was an adulterer, and
murdered Urias? Does all this sound too hotly?
I suppose an honest man is bound to keep quite cool
when he hears his mother dubbed harlot.

PROGRESS AND PERFECTION

DIFFERENT sorts of accusations are thrown at the Catholic Church by different sorts of people; and the accusations of one age are not always identical with those of another. Thus, many of the calumnies of old-fashioned Protestantism against Catholicity are no longer much attended to by a society that has escaped almost as far from the Protestant standpoint as it has from the Catholic: that the old religion of Christendom is honeycombed with superstition that society is prepared to believe without subjecting itself to the *ennui* of proof; but it does not think the point very interesting or important, for, having made up what it is pleased to call its mind that *all* Christianity is a moribund, if not defunct, superstition, it hardly finds it worth while to consider closely invidious comparisons between one form of the superstition and another. It may, indeed, and often does, take up the position that if people are still quaint enough to go on believing in a religion that teaches the Incarnation of God, the Virginal Birth and the Resurrection of Christ, they may as well go the whole hog, and believe all that the Catholic Church teaches; and they perceive a greater picturesqueness in the unmitigated ancient

faith of Rome than in the half-hearted compromise
of a Protestantism that accepts what they consider
impossibilities while jibbing at miracles, or accepts
miracles up to a certain date, and angrily discards
as impostures all similar phenomena subsequent to
the period when decent, God-fearing Protestant
miracles thought it time to stop taking place.

This attitude is on the increase among non-believers who are free from violent rancours against
supernatural religion, and content themselves with
a placid surprise that so primitive a foible should
survive in any shape; obsolete survivals are not,
they admit, uninteresting; and the more antique the
more curious are such reminders of a state of things
which these superior persons imagine to have
passed away for ever.

The attitude is not quite so respectful as it is
sometimes assumed by the more simple-minded
Catholic to be; he is apt to imagine that it implies
a sort of involuntary tribute to the Church, as
though those who adopt it were confessing that,
after all, there *was* something in her that extorted
their admiration and compelled their respect.   The
admiration, when there is any, is only what an
aesthetic socialist might feel for the fine ruins of a
feudal stronghold; the respect not much deeper than
a young graduate of London, who has just taken
honours in natural science, may feel called upon to
render to a septuagenarian Oxford don still irritat-
ing himself over a disputed reading in Theocritus.
It is not necessarily a proof of a wider mind, and

may only evince a shallower feeling; it certainly need not be taken as a sign of readiness to consider the Church's claims on their merits, but may merely express the conviction that such questions are settled and done for—"Quaestio finita est, Romana damnata est."

Such critics, then, as these will never fatigue themselves by loud shoutings of the sort of hoary accusation dear to the true Protestant heart: a pother about sacraments or indulgences, purgatory and saints, seems to them a storm in a tea-cup, and they are sure the tea-cup itself is cracked and cannot hold even the most mildly agitated milk and water. And Gallio is apt to be a smooth-mannered fellow. He does not noisily revile, nor call names that are universally felt to be insulting. To scream and vituperate is vulgar, and degrades the accuser. He does not run amuck against wind mills. That is foolish. But he accuses, too, though in the measured tone of dispassionate, because impregnable, criticism.

Interesting as the venerable institution of Catholicity is, striking as her objective personality undoubtedly remains, grandiose as have been the spectacles with which she has decorated the stage of history, noble as have been many of her aims—far before the times as some of them clearly were—exalted as was the mission she set herself, great as was the part she once played in civilising the savage nations that were too virile to assimilate so effete a civilisation as that of the Roman Empire, sick and

dying, fine as were the ideals she displayed to mankind in comparison with any that had been promulgated before her time, she is, alas! an enemy to
Progress.   She is the latter-day Canute, with her
throne upon the shore of time, opposed to the on-
rush of a tide inexorably advancing to submerge
it; but, unlike Canute, forbidding its advance with
a fatuous sincere desire of being obeyed.   Her
throne, indeed, was planted, as she avers, not upon
the low and shifting sand, but upon a rock—the in-
tensely significant, picturesque Peter-rock; but she is
unable to perceive that the rock itself (owing to
the erosion of time) is now below high-water mark,
and if she persists in remaining in her ancient seat
she must find herself overwhelmed.   They profess
a half-regret: if only she would get up and run in-
land, leaving all her *impedimenta* behind—her dog-
mas and her weird claims, her fantastic fooleries,
that did well enough for a world in its fairy-story
stage, her baubles that pleased children who had not
got beyond coral-mumbling—she might fit herself in
with meek usefulness to some subordinate part in a
society that has still a good many poor members.
What could she do better than lay aside her old
arrogant part of heaven-sent teacher, and assume
the eminently practical function of State-provided
relieving officer?   She has, they readily concede, "a
way wid her," and has seemed to understand how
to deal with pauperism better than her more en-
lighted successors, the administrators of poor laws.
When she ruled the roost poverty was not so crim-

inal nor so menacing as it is latterly become. Let her lay down her triple crown and take office under the beneficent masters who have paternally cut her throat, and a wide sphere, unversed by tedious puerilities of belief, will be opened for her grand-motherly (for she is very old) and innocuous good nature.

But she will not: so she is an enemy to Progress. She sticks to her old claims, and clanks her old chains, like the bothersome ghost she is—a ghost with an immense body, which makes her abnormal and inexcusable even among ghosts. She is dead and will not be buried, but stalks about galvanically, like a duck whose head was of so little account that she cannot realise it has been cut off. The Papacy is her head, and it was cut off in 1870, not to tire oneself with earlier decapitations. Her behaviour is more scandalous than the duck's, for the body ran back to the head, and refused to admit the fact of decapitation, maintaining the same phenomena of life as if no operation at all had taken place. That is the worst of the Catholic Church, it *is* a phenom-enon, and persists in a world that can only away with phenomena that are natural or preternatural, and finds its delicacy outraged by the naked supernat-ural. The whole spirit of the age is progressive, and the Catholic Church is the only considerable in-stitution that refuses to take its colour from the age, adopt the current axioms, discarding her own, and proclaim as her objects those which the rest of the world acknowledges to be the only ones worth aiming at.

This is *their* accusation: that the Church is effete, because out of touch with the aspirations of society; and really mischievous because, so far as her power goes, she retards progress and is in opposition to it. Like some other accusations against her, it is false in statement, but witnesses to a misapprehension of a truth that exists. The aspirations of the age may be discordant from those of the Church, and yet she is no enemy to Progress. For progress she has always been working, and is working still, over all the world, in the heart of each of her children who will listen to her urgent voice.

If they who bring the charge could arraign her before their tribunal they would smoothly warn her that she was on her defence.

"But you have no counsel: to that you are entitled."

"I need none. He whose Voice I echo in this world is the Prince whose name is called Councillor. It suffices me. But there *is* a difficulty: our language is not the same. I know what yours means, but you do not understand mine. You accuse me of desiring to bar Human Progress."

"Do you deny it?"

"What do you mean by Progress?"

"Movement."

"In what direction?"

"Forward of course."

"Is not all movement forward in some direction? Does not every step carry him who moves towards something, and is not it, therefore, a movement forward towards that thing, whatever it is?"

"You are quibbling.   Can you really not understand us?"

"I can understand you; but I want you to express your meaning."

"We mean, then, by Progress, movement forward towards the betterment of society."

"I have been toiling for its betterment during nearly nineteen centuries."

"You used to do so.   We know all you have done in the past.   It was much.   But your clock has stopped, and its hands stand still."

"They point to-day as they have pointed always."

"Whither?"

"To Eternity."

(A slight movement of impatience on the part of the Examiners).

" 'Eternity.'   But Eternity is not our affair."

"No.   It is mine."

"Our business is with men, and they belong to Time."

"They belong to Eternity: a little bit of Time belongs to them—not by right, but by gift.   It is lent to them to work with—while it is called to-day."

"Ah, 'to-day'!   That is more practical.   It is with to-day we concern ourselves."

"And so do I: and with yesterday—for warning

and for learning; and with to-morrow—for hope."

"You deal too much in hope—and promises."

"They are not mine. He who makes them keeps them. It is my office to remind of them, lest they be forgotten."

"You speak of God. It is of man we wish to speak. We leave God to you."

"But I cannot keep Him to myself; He does not belong to me, but I to Him, and all men are His: if I tried to keep Him to myself I should be a thief like you."

"We do not keep Him to ourselves."

"No. You steal Him from the world, as far as you can; not for yourselves, but to destroy Him—if you could."

"You wander from the point—you are very old, and age is discursive."

"My point is always the same—God; and I have never wandered from it. You call me old because I have lived long; I was alive nearly two thousand years before you, and I shall be alive when you are dead. But old age is feeble, and has dull hearing and dim sight, and has no fertility, and chill feet, and palsied hands—"

"You *will* wander. It was of Human Progress we were to speak."

"And I told you that you could not understand me, though I can understand you better than you seem able to express yourselves."

"You talk arrogantly—an old fault of yours."

"It sounds arrogant, in the ears of them who are

not certain, when one who *is* certain says what she means."

"We are certain that you oppose yourself (ineffectually, of course) to the progress of mankind."

"I reminded you how I helped it—"

"Yes, and we admitted it. That point was conceded. Let us get on, it is tiresome arguing round and round."

"I did not know you were arguing. I thought you only seemed to be asserting."

"Come! You keep harking back to the past; it is excusable, for you belong to the past—"

"I must interrupt you: part of the past belonged to me, for I lived in it, and helped to fashion it when it was the present. But I am alive still, and have my share in the present that now is."

"No. That is our contention—you turn your back on the present, and abdicate it. You do not belong to the living world."

"Then I am dead. And you are wasting your breath on a corpse! I thought you said you were practical. Are you a sort of spirit-rappers, fooling in a dark room with bogies?"

"Now you are flippant. In elderly persons it is more comely to be serious."

"I am cheerful. You are dismal—it is the fashion of your age, and I do not wonder."

"We have nothing to be dismal about. We, the heirs of all the ages—"

"But the inheritance of the ages you discard.

Heirs who made themselves penniless are often anxious and melancholy."

"That is nonsense. We have all that the experience of untold ages has accumulated."

"Except God."

"Why will you keep bringing Him in? You seem to have only one idea."

"That is so. But it comprehends everything."

"We must agree to differ. How you elude the point! Human Progress: if only you could stick to it."

"I am not its bar. It is only one of the jewels in my crown."

"You claim sovereignty still! You prate of crowns."

"My crown is not regal, but vice-regal—"

"Ah, we see what you would be at! Back again to the old tedious point. Will you answer our accusation?"

"Formulate it."

"That you are the arch-foe of Human Progress."

"That is not formulation, but repetition; that may be tedious without having precisely a point."

"You oppose Liberty."

"Do I? Whence came the idea? Who first taught the world that slave and sovereign had to render the same account before the same tribunal?"

"The past again! But who, in the present state of things, claims that every and all, and every man in it, is subservient to the same irresponsible authority?"

"God."

"That name again! But it is commonly believed that you claim this subservience for *yourself.*"

"Commonly believed! Vulgarly believed, by the ignorant and vulgar. Are vulgar beliefs so sacred to you? I claim nothing for myself but everything for my King—Whose viceroy in this world I am."

"You claim that every intellect should bow to your decree."

"God claims that the mind of every man who knows a little should bow to His that knows all."

"We cannot deal with you while you identify yourself with Him. Can you not answer for yourself?"

"I have no self apart from Him. My existence depends on His. I have no independent being. I am His Church; if He is not, I am nothing; that is why you call me dead—because you imagine He is abolished."

"Subtleties!"

"Simplicities! You have always accused me of subtlety. It is my simplicity that disconcerts you— and always will. That the Church has no independent existence, but depends on God's is what annoys you. I *am,* only because He *is;* and, since you want to say He is not, and never was, I am the most unpardonable thing in a world that pretends that He is nowhere. If I were what you say I am, I should have ceased long ago."

"Such as you are, you are a fact—"

"Certainly. A witness, too; and a witness that can never be cajoled, nor silenced, nor ignored.

That is my crime.   You cannot disbelieve God and suffer me patiently."

"You talk of ideas that are superannuated.   But, though you, too, are superannuated, there you are."

"You mean here."

"Very well, here.   You always loved fiddling with words."

"On the contrary, my habit is not to let words fiddle away truth: I will not suffer them to skip about, but bind them to a meaning, and see what it comes to.   You say I am here; that is your real grievance against me.   You *know* I am alive, and you know I could not be if God were dead.   Extinct monarchies have no viceroys.   You are angry because you pretend God is gone, and you cannot pretend I am extinct.   I am His moon, and my reflected light is intolerable to you because you run about saying the sun is quenched.   My existence is offensive to you because it is an incorruptible witness to the survival of a Lawgiver Whose laws you do not want to obey."

"We bow to the inexorable law of Human Progress."

"If it be an inexorable law it must be obeyed without your help.   Your interference and assistance must be superfluous and officious—as if you were to make it your business to enforce the laws of gravitation."

"You are garrulous—like all old persons. The point is that you set yourself against His law."

"If there be such law, who made it?"

"We know what you would be at: but it is self-existent."

"Then it must be divine. Perhaps you worship it. If so, it is unfortunate that your god lacks the attribute of omnipotence."

"Perhaps it does not lack it."

"If it be omnipotent the law of Human Progress can lose nothing by the opposition you attribute to me."

"Does your God lose nothing by our not obeying Him?"

"He has all things."

"Except our obedience and recognition."

"Your obedience and recognition which do not exist are not things. Non-existences are nothing."

"That is how you love to talk. Will you or will you not, say whether you do oppose Human Progress."

"I know that I have never opposed it. But you have never yet told me what you mean by it."

"Yes, we have. We have told you we mean by it the betterment of man."

"To make man better means to make him more good. That is my endless task."

"Oh, 'good!' You are there, are you? We know pretty well what you mean by good—"

"You may well know. I have never made any secret of it. But you speak slightingly when you talk of goodness—"

"Of your sort of goodness."

"What is your sort?"

"We do not hold a man good who merely says many prayers—"

"Nor do I."

"You make a great deal of it."

"I *think* a great deal of it. It is a help towards being good."

"You think so. We do not. We think a man good who fulfils every duty—"

"Your good men must be few."

"Especially all his duties towards mankind."

"Every man is himself a part of mankind. Has he any duties towards the rest of it?"

"We never said so. You try to put words in our mouths—"

"No. I am only trying to fit some meaning to your words. What are a man's duties towards himself?"

"They are many: to be sober, for instance, and honest and truthful."

"They *are* his duty. Why?"

"Do you not know?"

"Very well. But, if you know too, why not say?"

"Insobriety, dishonesty, and lies are sins against society."

"Sins against one's neighbour. That is true. But we were talking of a man's duty to himself. Mind, I am well aware these things *are* sins against a man's self. I am glad you think so, too. But you have merely alluded to their being offences against society, as they certainly are. And I should like to hear why you believe them offences against a man's self."

"Because every man should be a blameless member of society."

"That seems rather because of his duty towards society."

(One Examiner): "Man has no existence except as a unit in society."

(Another Examiner, to him): "Take care, I am afraid she will catch hold of that; besides I am not sure if it is true."

(She, to the first Examiner): "If that be so I do not see how any individual man can have private duties to himself."

(First Examiner): "In this way. Each self belongs to society and the betterment of society involves the betterment of self."

"That still leaves what you call betterment a public duty. I cannot see quite where your private duties come in."

"No, there are no private duties. Every duty is public, to the body of mankind."

"If private duties do not exist, I do not perceive how private sins can exist. Is there any harm in private, undetected drunkenness?"

"Of course. The man would be a private blackguard; if all society consisted of private blackguards it would be a blackguard society."

"I quite agree with you. But if a man should happen to see no harm in being drunk, so long as no one knows and no one is annoyed?"

"That does not alter facts. He is a blackguard all the same."

"I agree again. You mean he breaks a law, and the fact that he is not detected does not alter the other fact that the law is broken."

"Precisely."

"But who made the law of sobriety?"

"Ah! you would, would you? We know what you are driving at. But the law of sobriety is a law of nature."

"Is nature conscious? I do not understand how what is impersonal can be; nor how what is unconscious can enact laws. Perhaps I do not understand what you mean by nature."

"Very likely. Nature is the whole universe and the laws that govern it."

"You identify the universe and its laws. The imposition of a law implies superiority, not identity; nothing can be superior to itself."

"You are striving to entangle us in metaphysics. We wish to talk plain common sense."

"I wish you would. Will your common sense mind explaining how Nature has laws made by herself?"

"It is the simple fact."

"To say that the point in discussion is a simple fact may be true or false, but it is not explanation. You say the laws of nature are made by nature."

"Yes."

"Then she obeys them merely because she choses, and is free to disobey them."

"Nature cannot infringe her laws."

"Then they are not hers, but are imposed by a power higher than hers. No self-made law is obligatory; it is merely a resolution of self-guidance. If what you call laws of nature have no obligation on nature, they cannot bind the different parts of which she is a whole. Mankind is a part, and each man is a part of mankind; if there be no law but that of nature, he, a part of it, may say, 'This law of mine is tiresome. I dispense myself from it. It is only a resolution of my own, and to keep it bores me'."

"Now you are arguing for immorality."

"No I am not. I am stating facts. If morality be not inherent it implies a law to enforce it. If it be inherent there can be no immorality, for by inherent necessity morality will subsist impregnably uninfluenced by any person's conduct. If, however, it be not inherent, but depends on correspondence to a law, then the law must have a sanction higher than that of the individual, or of the nature which he represents, of which he is a part and a constituent. If there really be a law of nature, it must be enacted by something higher than nature, else she need not obey it. If by laws of nature you mean laws enacted by nature herself, then man, if he be bound to obey, is not a part of nature, but something lower than her, and therefore distinct from her."

"We are getting tired. Will you flatly say whether you care for Human Progress? We know you do not, that you dislike, suspect, and fear it. Plead guilty or not guilty."

"You expect me to formulate the charge against myself. Your flatulent talk has never defined Human Progress. I will define your meaning for you. Your object is to make men more comfortable."

"Well."

"I cannot congratulate you on your success. Comfort is your ideal, not happiness. But even comfort ('scorned of devils,' as your poet sings), how much have you achieved in giving it? Is it because men are more comfortable than ever that they kill themselves more than ever? Your idea of supreme discomfort is poverty. When was there more of it? My object is not yours. I do not confound comfort and happiness. I can gild discomfort and make it happy—by the golden rays of indestructible Hope. You scorn hope, and can see nothing beyond the present; and how your votaries complain of it. Your fatuous endeavour is to provide sufficient comfort to go round, no matter who suffers. Mine is to lead all men to Perfection. This is my business: by a perfect example I woo all who will be brave to an ideal beyond your highest, wildest flight. You offer a few instalments of dull comfort; I summon all to Perfection—"

(The Examiner, laughing and interrupting): "Perfection!!!"

(A rustle and twitter of giggling merriment, much nudging and shrugging. . . .)

OF PREACHING AND PRACTICE

CATHOLICS who live in a non-Catholic country as we do in England, must, if they be worth the name of Catholic, not only desire very earnestly the conversion of their non-Catholic neighbours, but be much preoccupied by the thought of it. Converts may, naturally, feel this preoccupation with a special intensity, because those of whom they are thinking, for whom they are so constantly praying are their own flesh and blood—the parents by whom God gave them life itself, the brothers and sisters with whom they played in childhood, husband even or wife. Not to yearn for their conversion would seem, in their case, a lack of natural affection. And remembering by what roads they themselves arrived in the City of God's Peace they cannot but feel eager to show those roads to the dear ones they have left wandering outside. So that, to the captious Catholic of dull sympathies and sluggish imagination, they sometimes appear to "think too much of Protestants."

But though the convert may have this eagerness for the conversion of those still alien to the Church in a peculiar degree and though in him it may have a special vehemence of expression, no Catholic who really cares for his faith and knows the treasure he has in it can be at all indifferent in the matter.   And the more earnest a Catholic is about his religion, the farther will he be from anything like indifference. Accordingly, we find that some of those who in England have been most eager and devoted in the work of the spread of the Faith have been what are called "old Catholics," whose own kith and kin and ancestors had always been Catholic.

These have been willing to bear constantly in mind the missionary character of the Catholic Church in modern England.   They have warmly welcomed every prudent proposal that seemed in any way calculated to promote a knowledge of the Faith among non-Catholics; their own labour they have not spared; and they have displayed the most singular readiness of sympathy in their endeavour to prejudices of those outside.
understand and fit themselves to the ideas or even

Without pausing upon great and famous names, like those of Wiseman and Ullathorne, we may truthfully say that the work of the conversion of England up to the present time has largely been carried on by Irish priests and Irish nuns in England in spite of the extreme divergence of *natural* sympathies and feelings beween them and the Anglo-Saxon people with whom they have had to deal. And nothing could more marvellously illustrate the constraining force of grace, the wonderful results that the sheer love of God, and of man for God's

sake can effect: for the national difference of
character, apart altogether from accidental dif-
ferences such as occur in the mere region of political
ideas, is, as I think, much greater between an Irish-
man and an Englishman than that between an
Englishman and a German, or an Englishman and a
member of one of the Latin races.

In spite, I say, of this natural divergence, almost
antipathy, of character, I have never known an Irish
priest in England who did not love the English
members of his flock and was not loved by them in
return with just as true a filial devotion as if he had
been an Anglo-Saxon like themselves.

Accordingly at the present moment, when the
bulk of the Catholic clergy in England is still Irish
by birth, or by name and descent, every plan or
movement for what is called the conversion of England is welcomed and adopted by the clergy with
untiring hope and a self-sacrificing readiness to lend
their own, already hugely overtaxed, labours to it.
Nor, on the whole, are they badly seconded by the
laity; for it is hardly fair to expect the laity
to behave like missionary priests: and a great pro-
portion of the Catholic laity in England do seem to
realize that *their* position too has, in a country like
this, some missionary character.

It is not at all my present purpose to speak of the
various organizations we have for the spread of
Catholic truth—or, in other words, for the conversion of England; I do not want to detail them, or
express at large the admiration I feel for the noble

work they are doing. I merely wish to recognise their existence, and record my full sense of their necessity, to rejoice in all they are doing and bid God-speed to them, one and all.

Apart from any such societies there is another sort of work that is being done for the spread of Catholic truth—the work of preaching and of writing; sometimes by the same brilliant and zealous men, though sometimes the preaching is done by one set of Catholic apologists, and the writing by another. In both cases it is being done very well. The pity is that the Catholic sermons are not heard and the Catholic books not read by more of those for whose sake in especial they are preached and written. We can only help both preacher and writer by our prayers that, by what men call accident, more hearers from outside may accrue to the preachers and more readers to the writers; and by our prayers that God Himself may guide those who make the sermons and the books, that they may say and write what may best help to set out the beauty and truth of the Catholic faith and ideal of human life.

This much is put down here lest it should for a moment seem as though I thought any of these things, the societies, the sermons, or the books and writings, anything short of indispensable. We need not less of them all, but more and more. Yet there is something else. The ultimate cause of any conversion to the Catholic Church has lain, not in any society, in any preacher, in any writer, but in the truth of that expressed by the society, the sermon, or the book.   In other words, it is the Church herself that converts outsiders, not her exponents.   If the Church were not what the society, or the sermon, or the book pretended, it would be found out, and conversions would not follow on any organization, or any eloquence, or any brilliance of literary exposition.

Heresy and unbelief have decried and defamed the Church: the enquirer may take note of what this or that society urges upon his attention, of what such a preacher argues, what such a book pleads, but he goes behind all of them, and considers for himself the evidence provided by what, in fact, Catholics are made by the Catholic Church to be.

There are converts, no doubt, who have been, so to speak, converted by their reading, in their studies; by weighing of historical, philosophical, and ethical proofs and arguments; by whom the past is called up to bear witness, from whom the august story of the Church's influence, of her claims and of her defence of them, has been the guiding beacon that led them to the City on the Hill; and such converts have been among the most influential.   *Their* conviction has convinced others in turn.   But they have never been, or can be, the majority; and incalculably beneficial as their conversions have been, directly or indirectly, not only to those under the direct influence of their personality or of their writing and preaching, but upon the general estimation of the Catholic body by those outside it, there remains the fact that there is a class much more numerous than the reading class, and a non-Catholic public that never enters a Catholic church or hears a Catholic preacher, incomparably more numerous than that mere percentage that does occasionally hear a Catholic sermon, and may, as it were, at haphazard read some Catholic work.

By what means, humanly speaking, are such people to be brought to the consideration of the claims of Catholic truth?   On what, in other words, can we ground any human hopes of their conversion —since we can hardly be content if only the student or the religious expert is to be converted?

The answer lies in the consideration of the influences that *have* drawn such people, in the first instance at all events, that *are* drawing many such, every day, up and down the country, to give the necessary initial attention to the claims of the Catholic Church; for until that attention be caught nothing further can be done.   Apart, then, altogether from the more intellectual type of convert, whose own study brings him to recognise Catholic truth, it is certain that immense numbers, to whom religious study appeals as little as any other study, have become Catholics by the force, in the first instance, at any rate, of Catholic example.   Such people have had Catholic friends, relations, or acquaintances; and, wholly without knowledge, as they have been, of anything like dogma or of history, they have been able to perceive in the Catholics they knew something that made them aware of a genuineness, a reality, in the religion of those Catholics that was novel in their experience. The Catholics themselves, hard-working, poor, with little leisure and perhaps with little taste for anything like study, may not have been experts in the theory of their religion, or of its history; nevertheless, they did know what they believed, what they did not believe, and what they might not believe; their faith was not vague, halting, wavering or inconsistent, but compact and definite, clear and capable of intelligible statement. And, furthermore, their practice was unmistakably directed by their belief. Their religion, while resting on a certain and articulate faith, expressed its conviction of professed truths in a consistency of conduct and conscience, also somewhat novel to these observers; for many an observer, grossly ignorant himself even of elemental religious truth, is shrewd enough in recognizing reality and consistency.

I believe that if the priests who receive into our Church, as they are daily doing all over England, the unlettered converts I am trying to describe, would give their evidence, it would be found to support what has just been urged: that is to say, that the majority of such converts were first drawn to consider Catholicity at all by the example of the Catholics they knew—of their own unlettered class. That example, the visible instances within their own rather narrow experience, first led these non-Catholics to surmise that the Catholic Faith does something for its members that no other religion does.

What struck them first was the easily-noted fact that these Catholic neighbours of theirs *cared* much more for their Church than any other people they knew seemed to care for theirs. They perceived in Catholics an affection for Catholicity that was singular in their experience. For, among the masses belonging nominally to the Established Religion of England, any thing that could be called personal affection for the Church of England is very unusual: the most of them would be inclined to give no stronger reason for belonging to it than that they did belong to it, and might as well belong to it as anything else. And the other masses, perhaps more really numerous, that belong to the various Nonconformist bodies, seem to do less out of a peculiar love to their own sect than out of a dislike or suspicion of the Establishment; their adhesion seems to have chiefly a negative, rather than a positive, significance: they belong there because they refuse to belong somewhere else. When most heated it is not with love for their own body but with anger against, or disapproval of, the body from which they seceded.

Of the beauty and sweetness of their own particular Free Church, of its credentials and its noble history, they have little to say in comparison with what they have to bring in accusation against the elder heresy from which they broke away: its deadness, Erastianism, worldliness, unspirituality, tyranny, or corruption. The value of their own sect is rather urged comparatively than positively, and the measure of their fondness for it is chiefly the degree of their animosity against that whence they cast themselves loose. And this attitude expresses itself very well in vehemence and invective, but is much less eloquent in eulogy; it finds itself warm and glib in criticism, but more chilly in the language of love.

And such observers as I am trying to describe, shrewd though not much lettered or expert, can fully note this, and can contrast it with the *positive* affection of Catholics, simple as themselves, for their own Church. The Catholics, they perceive, have a love for their religion which is not merely comparative; they love their Church for what she is, not simply because she is not some other body that they dislike and have a grudge against: they would much rather talk of the glories of the Church than of the failure of other religions to achieve such glories. If our observer sometimes begins to tell himself that his Catholic friend seems a little disposed to brag of the greatness of his Church, he also suspects that the other religionists are not so modest but what they would be equally inclined to boast of the glories of *their* sect if they were equally able to state in what those glories consisted; whereas they appear somewhat inclined to leave those splendours to the imagination of their hearer—duly inflamed by abuse of the counsel on the other side.

If, he is able to perceive, his Catholic friends do assume a somewhat lofty tone in talking of the wonders of the Catholic Church, they at least are ready to say what those wonders are; they have a long list of actual possessions to detail, and the spiritual riches of the Catholic Church do not merely consist in the spiritual poverty of the rival religions: if there *were* no rival bodies the Catholic Church would evidently be not a penny the poorer; but where would the magnificence of Nonconformity be if there were no Church of England?

Our shrewd and simple observer confesses that, if the Catholic also dislikes the schismatic religions, it is obviously because, in his estimation, they have intervened to deprive Christians of their heirloom in all that should have been theirs in the Church; whereas the schismatics abhor the Church, not for having stolen something away, but for keeping intact what they hoped to have destroyed; for insisting on giving to men what they have assured mankind it does not in the least require. And our observer notes that all these things that the Catholics still have, which their Church goes on giving them, unperturbed by the outsider's cry that they are useless and mischievous, are highly valued by them who still have them, and do, somehow, make them Christians of a more distinctively Christian quality, and give them an unmistakable character of supernatural, definite, unwavering, unworldly, unpagan religion that is not elsewhere observable. He perceives that a Catholic is, at all events, not at all like a rationalist, an unbeliever, or a decorously-dressed heathen; that Jesus Christ is to him God and law; that fashions in ideas do not send him peering about in search of principles; that on the voyage of life he

has his place in an ancient but not untrusted boat,
his pilot, and his chart; that he does not stand knee-
deep in the surf begging it to abstain from submerg-
ing him, nor clutching hold of every mass of drift-
wood, weed, or wreckage, and begging it to be his
vehicle some-whither.

It will be noted that allusion has so far been made
to two classes or grades of converts—those who,
before joining the Church, have made considerable
study of religious and ecclesiastical questions, and
those who have made very little, being in this latter
case the sort of people who are not in the way of
study of any kind. There are, of course, intermediate classes. There are the moderately educated,
and with these also the first impulse towards the
Church has often sprung from observation of Catholics, and the influences just described have affected
them in the same manner. Moving in a somewhat
higher social class, the Catholics they have known
have been better educated, and perhaps have been
able to give a more explicit account of their religion,
its creeds and its credentials. Nevertheless, it has
not been by what they have been able to say that
their non-Catholic friends have been drawn to give
some serious and respectful attention to Catholicity,
so much as by what the non-Catholics have perceived
them to be; it is as examples of Catholicity that they
have been mainly influential. Where the Catholic
is of absolutely first-rate quality this influence is very
great indeed; but the influence is considerable even
in the case of quite an ordinary Catholic, provided

he be a genuine, practising Catholic at all.   There
is something in this latter also which shows him to be
markedly unlike the nominal Christian, and like
nothing else except his fellow-Catholics.   And it is
plainly apparent that all that is best in him is due
to the fact of his religion; it is not attributable to
merely personal qualities, and cannot be mistaken
for the effect of individual character.   An outside
observer soon notes that, with Catholics, the more
Catholic they are the better they are; and this he
does not perceive in the case of members of other
religious bodies; whence he concludes that there is
something in Catholicity that tends to excellence in
its members.   So strongly does this principle impress
itself upon him that, afterwards, you will find him
little disposed to accuse the Church of the faults of
bad Catholics; for he has come to know that the
more faulty they are the less are they under the influence of their faith.   Nevertheless, it remains
true that if he had, in the first instance, been so unfortunate as to come across only bad Catholics, he
would have been very little drawn to any respectful
consideration of Catholicity.   He might have tacitly
assumed them to be ordinary specimens of what the
Church makes of her children; as it is, he takes
them for bad specimens.   Even here, however, it
is fair to remark that many a very imperfect Catholic, of irregular life and lax practice of his religion,
does somehow bear witness not merely against himself but in favour of his religion; against himself by
being what he is; in favour of his neglected faith by

oddly showing what it would do for him if he would let it. Until he has lost his faith altogether, even the careless Catholic has commonly something about him that reminds us of the spiritual inheritance he is wasting; however dormant or ill-treated, there is in him a supernatural sense that will often strike a brother-scapegrace.

All that I have been trying to say comes, then, to this: that it is *the Church herself that converts*, in innumerable instances, rather than any eloquence of a preacher, or any arguments of a writer, or any efforts of a society. It is the inherent quality of Catholicism that arrests the observer, and disposes him to consider the other evidences of its truth.

From this it is not at all intended to deduce the maxim that we are to seem as good as possible; that we are to behave smugly and pretend that Catholics are all good; that all the professors of any religion have ever been exemplary. I suspect that some harm is done by the over-eager zeal of some good people who will never admit that a Catholic has been seriously at fault. Nobody's eyes are opened by our trying to throw dust in them, however loyal our intention may be, and to try is really not an overflow of faith but a defect of it. The Church has nothing to lose by the whole truth being known; it is the blindness of those outside she has to heal, not any keenness of their scrutiny. Catholic dirty linen, it is urged by weaker brethren, should never be washed in public; that is really a question of taste, and dirty linen anywhere is obnoxious to a taste that is refined. But what is of substantial consequence is that there should be as little dirty linen as possible to need washing, and that depends not on history but on ourselves. In other words, the quality of the Catholic body depends upon its members; let them see to it. That is every Catholic man's share in the conversion of the non-Catholic world. Some may write, some may preach, some may organise, but all must *be;* and on what we *are* will rest the conclusion of the outside world as to the effects of Catholicity upon the Church's children.

That is why I would urge the general recognition of Catholics that the conversion of England, or of any non-Catholic society, will not really be effected by preaching, or writing, or organising, though each is necessary, and an obedience that we owe to Our Lord's mandate; but by the Church being what she is; and our own share in proving what she is, must lie in making ourselves what she wishes us to be. Where, in any given region, the Church has suffered real loss, apart from material loss—as of endowment, patronage, establishment, etc.—her members in that region can hardly be excused from their share of responsibility for the evil; for though attacks come from without, and no excellence of the Church's children anywhere can disarm real malice and enmity, those attacks can only wound in material things, so long as the real substantial quality of the Catholic body in any region is what it ought to be. If we could suppose a region where the general quality of the Catholic body had fallen beneath itself, there, indeed, would the Church be liable to suffer grievous wounds in that one of her members. The Church herself is indeed indefectible, and we have Christ's promise that the gates of hell shall never prevail against her; but He has not promised that they shall not prevail against the unfaithful individual who, by disloyalty or failure to use the graces held for him in trust by the Church, abdicates his own share in the promise; and, in like manner, a special group of individuals, even so large a group as makes up the general body of Catholics in a given region, might by neglect of their religion bring it for the time almost to ruin there.

It requires no gift of prophesy to foresee that the present state and progress of things will before long make the Church, all over the world, what she was for many ages—the only representative of Christianity and of supernatural religion.

The purely natural forces of sectarian Christianity are being rapidly exhausted; they and their forbears had a certain capital of faith carried with them out of the Church into exile; on that capital they have been living, and it is nearly wasted; they have nothing, when it is gone, upon which they can go on living. For the life of religion is not indefinitely divisible, like some forms of natural life whose mode of propagation consists solely of progressive splitting up. The unresting splitting up of the sects does not increase their stock of life, but only wears it out.

As for the ancient schismatic churches, they are

not at all missionary or propagandist, and the unbelieving world is entirely uninfluenced by them.   So
that the Catholic Church will presently stand heiress
by default of the Christian faith and inheritance.
The sum of what she will be recognized by the world
to possess will largely depend upon the quality of
her members; each individual Catholic, therefore,
should feel his own responsibility, and in his own
life and person contribute his own offering to the
Church's spiritual, ethical wealth.   No Catholic is
to say to himself that the conversion of England,
or of any country, is the business of the writers, the
preachers, and theologians, the various organisa-
tions existing to that end in the Church; they are to
do their share, he is not to leave his share undone,
and his is to contribute to the quality of Catholicity
his own correspondence with the graces that the
Church is daily urging upon his acceptance.

If it were possible, as it is not, for the Carmelite
in her cell to read of some of the noble efforts being
made all over the Catholic world for the conversion
of heretics and unbelievers, can we not imagine that
she might feel a compunction, a scruple, a twinge, as
it were, of regret that in all these works she was not
sharing?   And yet it would be a scruple, and, like
all scruples, a false accusation, a pitiful attempt of
the Arch-Accuser to confuse issues and weaken
strength.   She would know it was so; the grace of
her sublime and unearthly vocation would teach her
to throw it from her with smiling trust and knowledge of God, Who sets one here and another

there, and never asks one to do another's work, or demands that the adept with one tool or weapon should bungle with another. She would know that God had given her a rare and special work for the world's conversion. And while she in her lowly estimation of herself, would remember, perhaps, only her prayers, we must remember much more. Though behind the grill that hides her perfection from all sight but God's no man ever hears her voice, or sees her face; though it be not hers to preach, nor hers to write; though her influence be unsuspected by the jostling, unpraying world outside; though she deliver no argument and speak of God only to Himself—yet she is doing much for the conversion of the world. Of her prayers we do not speak; such prayer as hers is *Sacramentum Regis,* the King's secret, a ground holy and ineffable, into which we dare not pry. But she does something else: she, out of sight, on the gaunt and austere heights of Carmel, is giving her quality to the Church. To its spiritual wealth she is, with lavish hand, contributing her daily, hourly gold; her thin hand drops more into the treasury than ours. And these gifts of hers are given by every religious of every Order. Of some the world itself takes cognisance, because their special function is to minister to the only wants the world can understand: sickness and poverty and gross ignorance. But, noble as all these works are, whether done by religious or seculars, by those dedicated openly to God's service in priesthood or cloister, or by the Catholic layman or woman, we, who are Catholics, must ever remember that it is not in their "utility" (as the world has it) that their sole glory lies; rather it is because all who share in such labours are contributing each his share or hers to the spiritual quality of Catholicity, that is, of the actual body Catholic.

Do all Catholics remember this? I myself have heard Catholics say of themselves: "*We* are workers. Your Carmelites, your Poor Clares, your Trappists, and the rest, what do they do?"

Should they not rather ask themselves what the Trappists and the Poor Clares and the Carmelites *are*? By what they are, these hidden servants serve. Giving *themselves* to God and His Church, they give more than any sermon can give, or any book, or any speech; it is by such gifts as theirs that the Church is held on a plane higher than that of the most restlessly energetic sect. It is they, and those who are like them, who make true the things we *say* about the Church and her ineffable, inimitable sanctity.

The sects can preach and talk and organise, so must we; but unless there is more behind us, we shall hardly be what we are to be if the world is still to see in the Church something wholly different from the sects, something marked with a higher and more divine impress, that intrinsic quality that in every age has convinced the world that Christ dwells in the Church at home, as He does not anywhere besides.

We must work; but the kingdom of God cometh

not with observation. There is a world to convert, and it means toil and thought and trouble; but it means more: that those who aim at a supernatural result must be supernatural themselves, and realise that their fellow-workers are not all visible on platforms, on committees, or even in pulpits, or to be heard in books and newspapers. The Church's claim lies in what she is, not in what the most eloquent tongue can say of her; it is a finer work to help in making true the best that could be said of her effect upon her children than to run about declaring what that effect is.

SACRAMENTS AND SPECTACLES

DURING many years of the Victorian age, England was indulged with very little in the way of public spectacle. The Great Exhibition was followed all too soon by the death of the Queen's Consort, and, though his widow relaxed nothing of her indefatigable attention to public affairs, and remained devoted as ever to work, she had lost heart for great ceremonial displays. During a period longer than many reigns her public appearances were few, and they were mostly surrounded with a minimum of state and splendour. London was almost left to its Lord Mayor's Show for gratification of the citizens' taste for spectacular effects.

But, almost suddenly, the last quarter of the old century and the first decade of the new saw a remarkable change: the two Jubilees were celebrated with an entirely new magnificence; there were many other great Royal functions; and then, in all too brief succession, followed two Coronations, to say nothing of the sad but grandiose ceremonial of the two Royal funerals.

Since 1887 it has appeared how fond the English people may become of show and spectacle, and that fondness has been indulged by a number of Royal functions, State or semi-State, and of other great displays, municipal and otherwise. The new England has been showing, in many ways, how much it likes to look at things—foreign fleets and potentates, Indian troops and princes, emperors, kings, presidents, and, now, the cinematograph.

'Tis a natural fondness, and no one should want to scold it. The Catholic Church has ever recognised its existence and has consistently indulged it in her own magnificence of ritual. Her mission is to make man what he should be, but she never aims at doing this by ignoring what he is. To do that latter thing is quite easy, and doing it may save a good deal of trouble: to behave as though men were angels, without passions or senses, requires no wonderful gifts; it only implies a lack of insight, and a certain dulness of sympathy. If, these lazy critics urge, men were truly spiritual, they would not need or desire a ritual of worship visible and audible; perhaps, but it is no matter of uncertainty that man, on the whole, has never yet given proofs of having attained to perfect spirituality; and the kindly Mother takes him as he is, while gently leading him on to what she would make him if he would suffer her. That he is no angel, of a purely spiritual being, she knows: he has eyes and ears, and he will fill both, for he has an eye-hunger and an ear-hunger, as well as the stomach-hunger that no one pretends should be ignored. She will not leave him coldly alone to fill eye and ear with nothing beautiful in which she has any share. There is, of course the clean beauty of Nature, with all her lovely infinitude of exquisite sights and sounds and smells; but the Church will not behave as if all men lived within reach of Nature's wealth, or as if all possessed a sense which no experience of theirs has ever awakened or fostered; millions of her children are penned in huge towns—she cannot leave *them* to guess of the beauty of the Creator by the glory of the things created; the first Author of beauty is lovelier than them all, but they can never see those things.   And yet, in them also lies the dormant sense of beauty and dignity of show: sunrise on sea or hill they never see, nor spring's rapture of resurrection, but they have eyes, too, and ears, though to them never comes the sound of the sea's song along the summer shore, the lark's hymn "from heaven's gate, or near it," the poignant ecstasy of nightingale from moonlit river-meads, the cry of pheasant, or love-croon of dove "from out the woven copse."   Shall she forget them?   Shall she hold herself with a proud affectation that all are rich, or set in the sweet heart of quiet country places: that fair spectacle and noble melody are not needful to the poor, or appreciable by them?   God's gifts of loveliness are given already, she cannot give them over again; she cannot heal man's dire necessity, or greed, or vanity, that drives him from them; what she can she does.   She surrounds the worship of Him with a tribute to His sovereignty.   His Eternal Majesty has a right to all that ephemeral royalty claims; and to render it, even in these outward things of sight and sound, is inevitable to her generous, loving loyalty. There is no pompous self-glorification in it all, no pride of her own; no one accuses the Viceroy of ambition in his splendid state, it is all meant for the far-away, invisible King. The representative, for the moment, of Imperial Majesty in India does not, by gorgeous spectacle of which he is the centre, render himself suspect of disloyalty or of ambitious vanity; he holds the Vice-regal seat to-day, another to-morrow, the real Emperor is distant but not forgotten, and all the splendour of his representative is but an evidence and reminder of his right and majesty. And so it is with the Church and her ancient, immemorial grandeur of ceremonial; it is all a part of a Vice-regal tribute to the King Eternal, and finds its supreme expression in the dignities of the King's Viceroy on earth, himself.

But while thinking first of God, and bearing tribute in all her ceremonial, in the first place, to His Majesty, the Church never forgets man, and to make him remember is her secondary, but great purpose. It is like the first and great commandment, and the other like to it. "But God needs no tribute such as this." What tribute does He *need*? Would He be God if He needed anything? Would they who urge this shallow plea against the solemnity of exterior worship declare that God would not be God if every soul were lost? Yet to save one soul He would not grudge His own death at the hands of the men He made? Should these little things be grudged if the common run of common men are helped even a little by them? Grant they are a condescendence to human infirmity—the Church is full of it; half her business is condescendence, and the other half encouragement. It is heresy that will not condescend, but bids man be an angel forthwith or accept the instant alternative of damnation. The Church is a Mother with every sort of child, and she will not shoulder out the imperfect, though the perfect reflect her inner mind and heart. Her patience has to last as long as the world, and the world is not yet a thing of the past. There are those who see God; but there are those who could never conceive of Him without a picture to hint of something in some one or two things suggestive of him—His power in one picture, His tenderness in another, His sovereignty here, His humility there, His awful self-sacrifice in the simplest of all. And of these folk she has a constant mind in all her year-long procession of ceremonial. By eye and ear she will lead them, by the heart as well as by the intellect. It is not her affectation to assume that man is a brain on two crutches. God's existence may be proved by reason, but man's salvation is not forced by any syllogism. He is "man and capable of his nature; few are angels;" he looks and listens. She will not scold him down and bid him argue only; she sets things before his eyes and fills his ear with sweet strains, that by those two homely avenues she may enter to his odd, man-filled, God-created heart. Her theory is to fill what else would be left vacant for this visible

world to fill up and occupy. For this condescendence
the heartless gibe at her; because man is half material, and even the material half she will preoccupy
for God if she can, she is dubbed material and un-
spiritual herself. Were the starven anchorites ma-
terialists—and who decries them? Is it the Church
that scoffs at Simeon on his pillar, at the gaunt her-
mit in his cave among the hills? It is not she who
insists that mortification of sense must mean misery;
it is not she who talks as though happiness were impossible to an un-indulged stomach. They who
scold her for indulging the material side of man by
her ceremonial worship are the same who condemn
her for not condemning her Carthusians; as though
materiality lay only in the eyes and ears, and the pal-
ate and stomach were purely spiritual organs.

She insists that God's grace can make man triumph over humanity itself; but she will not pretend
that human nature is in the main angelic. And to
human tastes she will condescend that by their means
also man may be led to think of God; the world has
its music for man's ears, she will have hers to carry
the name of God where else It might never come;
the world shall not have all the fine sights at which
men love to look, she must have hers to remind him
of another King, whose subjects they all are. Such
things are, urges the shallow, scornful critic, but
toys, and the grown man needs none. But this
Mother does not pretend that all her children are
grown up; the most of us attain our full manhood
only in eternity. And some of those who here are

proudest of their adult manliness lack the grace to
know how sacred a toy may be to a child.

But, though the Church indulges her children in
that taste for spectacles which nations allow themselves, she would be ill-satisfied were they to be
content with them. They are only a means to an
end: on the one hand a recognition of God's Sovereignty, and so a due act of homage from His lieges,
a reminder to them of their debt towards an in-
visible King; and on the other hand a condescendence to a very general need of men, by whose help
they may be lifted out of the flatness of dull or
common things to some remembrance of Eternal
beauty.

A nation may, however, become too fond of
pageants or fall into too dependent an indulgence
of its taste for them; and, should this happen, the
effect on national character would be enervating. A
people may become so given to spectacles, may
acquire so morbid a craving for the excitement of
watching games or shows, that it leaves its business
undone, or suffers others to do its business for it.

And individuals are subject to the same danger,
since nations are only very large groups of individuals, and what would hurt the big group will hurt
its members one by one.

The Church would not think him a satisfactory
Catholic whose religious acts consisted in watching
her ceremonial, as it were, from outside. He has
his business also, a spiritual business, to do *himself,*
and, should he absorb himself exclusively in an en-

joyment of ecclesiastical pageantry, he would be apt to leave that business undone, or trust to someone else doing it all for him.

The countless ceremonies of the Church's year are used best when they are used as a sort of sacramentals, but they can never be sacraments, or do the work of sacraments. And this some people are willing to forget. It is much easier to indolence to watch than to act, and far more congenial to a skin-deep spirituality to frequent ceremonies than to frequent the Sacraments. You will find many very willing even to carry something in a procession who want a great deal of persuading to go to Confession and Holy Communion. No doubt the taking part in the procession, even as onlookers, without carrying anything, does draw many to the Sacraments, partly by force, as it were, of mere reminder, partly by the operation of graces of which the procession is the occasion; but it is true also that some will take part in the procession without being moved to confess their sins and receive the Blessed Sacrament. That is not saying that in their case the taking part in the procession is quite useless, a merely empty, outward act, without any spiritual result: every religious act is good for religion; and among such acts there is an incalculable gradation—from that of the most perfect who takes part in it, down to that of the most imperfect: even in the lowest case the outward participation must serve as a reminder, must help to keep up a certain intimacy with the Church and her faith, must tend to ward off estrangement and coldness. And the Church will never quench the flax that only smokes. She will not obey the chill admonition of hard and unloving critics who cry out: "That fellow is not much of a Christian, even *your* Christianity he does not practise; he fights shy of your sacraments—and will only come to church when there is something fine to see; what business has *he* walking with a banner, or a torch, in his hand? Why do you not send him off?"

Were all they who cast their garments before Christ, and tore down branches from the way-side trees to strew His path withal, in the grace of God? Who can tell? But we know this, that He forbade none of them, and sent none of them coldly away. It may have been but an outward tribute with many of them, but He did not refuse or scorn it. Nevertheless, it is true that the Church wants her good things to be used in the best manner: she will snatch no crumb out of any mouth, but she longs to give fuller food. And the business of the faithful is to watch her upward-pointing finger without waiting for her hand to scourge. So that they who are content to indulge themselves with ceremonies, and hold still aloof from sacraments, are but dull children, surface-listeners whose ears are filled with sounds and keep hearts empty of their noble meanings; and silly, too, for it is a fool's part to grasp the pretty wrappings of a great gift, and fling the gift aside.

The wordly-wise are not imprudent thus, in their generation; when they know what is worth most, they will not seize what looks finest instead. But some of us are foolish fellows, and, because there is little show about a sacrament—how simple a thing is the giving of Holy Communion, how plain is the brief, Divine Word of Absolution!—we like better to walk in a procession, or take our ticket for a pilgrimage. Not, again, that we are to leave these last undone, but that we must not, on pain of blindness, leave the former undone.

Long ago a quiet voice said that they who go on many pilgrimages do not soon become perfect men. We know he did not mean that pilgrimage is not a special means of grace: but there are greater, and they lie to the hand of each, the poorest and the most home-bound. It would be odd indeed if God suffered the greatest means of grace to be the most costly—we know He does not—the most priceless cost nothing, and are as easy to the penniless as to the rich.

In some "Poor" Missions you shall hear those who love to excuse themselves complaining that there is not this or that; that some fair function they have seen elsewhere is not to be seen where they are; that some splendour of ritual, some richness of decoration, some magnificence of setting they have admired in another place, is lacking there—as if the ceremonial were more than its centre; as if Jesus Christ in the White Raiment of His Love-Prison depended for His Majesty on trappings that form no part of Himself. By no people is the patience of the most patient priest more hardly tried: they do not perceive that they are snobs of religion, though they are keen enough at noting the snobbery of those who are dazzled by the fine feathers of the world's fine birds, and think more of a man because his house or his clothes are sumptuous. They cannot, or will not, themselves remember that a king in a mean hovel makes a more potent appeal to real loyalty than when he is in his palace, surrounded with all the outward signs of majesty. They can condemn the sycophancy of earthly courtiers, that love to stand near jewelled thrones, while themselves are in the same case, holding aloof from their King till they can see Him in a grander place with finer things about Him.

MIRACLES—OR "SUCH-LIKE FOOLERIES"

COWPER, so far as I am aware, is the only writer of eminence who ever set down in black and white that the great lexicographer was a coxcomb, and it is probable he did not use the term in any of the senses attached to it by the doctor himself in his dictionary. For he could hardly have meant to call him either a "fop or a superficial pretender."

Most of us remember in what terms Macaulay speaks of Johnson's unreadiness to believe reports of extraordinary occurrences in the natural order, and of his credulity in the case of events of which there could be only a supernatural explanation. But, possibly, the great essayist did not quite appreciate the great lexicographer's point of view: Macaulay disliked the supernatural, and Johnson didn't. Johnson may have been willing to admit the truth of a supernatural occurrence the evidence for which would strike Macaulay as utterly insufficient; but then would Macaulay ever have admitted as sufficient the evidence for *any* event which could only be explained as being supernatural? No one is surprised if a man who believes all war to be unjustifiable decides at once on the injustice of any particular war of which there is question. Johnson was one of those to whom the unseen world is a reality as actual as anything the senses perceive: to him the world of spirits was not a phrase, but an immovable fact. And his mind was singularly reverent; nothing was more repugnant to it than the ordinary smug readiness to rule out whatever lies outside the mere limits of common experience. He could not admit that Omnipotence has nothing to do with modern life, or that what did not happen yesterday, and will probably not happen again to-morrow, cannot have happened to-day.

That some of the supposed circumstances which he was ready to believe might have occurred should rather be described as preternatural than supernatural may be true enough: but it is, perhaps, as true that Macaulay would have been as impatient of one as of the other: both, to his taste, would have been tarred with the same brush—the brush of impossibility. A ghost and a miracle would have annoyed him equally. No evidence would have convinced him of either, because both, in his estimate would be impossible.

The Catholic Church is not specially addicted to ghosts: if a census of them could be taken I suspect it would be found that the ghostly population of Catholic countries would be vastly out-numbered by that of Reformation countries. Scotland, England, the Scandinavian Kingdoms, and the Protestant States of Germany are thickly populated with ghosts. Rome is singularly deficient.

But then in Reformation countries they are free from miracles: you can't have everything. Scotland, in addition to its enormous ghostly population, has the second sight, and it was more generously supplied with witches till quite recent times than any other region in Europe, though Protestant New England ran it very close in the seventeenth and eighteenth centuries.

But if the Catholic Church is not peculiarly addicted to ghosts it is addicted to miracles. That is one of its spots, and, like the leopard, it will not change them, possibly for the same reason—the leopard did not invent his spots, but accepts them as a part of the Divine plan in his regard.

What is the real objection to miracles?

Why is it held so offensive a feature in the Catholic view of things that they are there "tolerated"? A belief in them—i. e., a belief that they can still happen, and do still happen—is still commonly assumed as an instance of the mental imbecility inherent in out and out Catholics: a proof of their uncritical, unpractical outlook on the world, of their inferior masculinity of intellect—in a word, of their superstitiousness.

Are "ghosts" then a distinctly Catholic institution? Are Catholics the only people who will not sit down thirteen to dinner; who are upset by seeing crossed knives on a table; who object to seeing the new moon through a window; who are pleased to see two magpies in a field but worried if they only see one; who touch wood to propitiate Nemesis when

they have boasted of good health or fortune; who
dislike dreaming of a wedding; who are complacent
when they bark their shins by falling upstairs, but
cross with the housemaid for meeting them there;
who will come down to breakfast, wreathed with
smiles of expectant prosperity, in a waistcoat inside
out, because they so put it on by genuine inadver-
tance; who throw rice and old shoes after a bride;
who used to carry a mutton-bone in their pocket to
keep off cramp; who wish when they pull a lucky
bone?

Is the second sight a Roman accomplishment or a
Scottish, and did the second sight disappear from
Scotland with the advent of the glorious Knox?
But all these superstitions have received Protestant
toleration, and why? Because they happen to be
merely unreasonable, and to have no justification by
faith. They are inexplicable by reason, and a
miracle is not: so they are pardonable and a miracle
isn't.

If you are pleased by seeing a compact group of
bubbles on the surface of your tea, and eat it with
your spoon, expecting money, you render no tribute
to Omnipotence: a little sacrifice on the world-old
altar of folly is merely amiable and prettily old-
fashioned. It is not simply old-fashioned to believe
in Omnipotence not obsolete, but a servile
recognition of a King in exile: to confess the
possibility of a miracle in the next street is to lift
the standard of an effete Power, as though you
should move back the clock to Israelitish days, when

a pillar of cloud by day, and a pillar of fire by night, proved to a people wandering in the Desert of Sin that they had a leader greater than Moses.

Archaism in itself is not objected to: but a form of archaism that must imply recognition of uncurtailed Omnipotence is thoroughly objectionable to the modern world.

The original attitude of non-Catholics was that of disbelief in *modern* miracles: only those recorded in the Bible could be admitted: but those recorded there must be believed. That position is rapidly being abandoned, for there is a Nemesis of logic more inexorable than that of fate. And the Catholic Church, which for centuries was assumed to be all against the Bible, and frightened of it, is quickly succeeding to the position of its heir by default: she will soon be the only champion of its integrity: she, who was supposed to weaken the splendour of the scriptural miracles by permitting rival miracles in modern life, will presently be the only defender of the reality and truth of those Bible miracles.

But those who will no longer believe in *any* miracles, because they have ceased to believe in Omnipotence, are often willing to believe in fooleries. Palmistry, Crystal-gazing, Astrology gain more and more adherents as faith loses them. It is not because a belief in miracles is unreasonable that such a belief is unpopular; for, admitting the existence of Omnipotence, the belief in them is simply reasonable and logical: the unpopularity of the belief is due to the fact that it is a part of the logic of faith. Nor is the belief in miracles scorned because it is superstitious; superstition lies in attributing effects to causes incapable of producing them and there is nothing superstitious in admitting that Omnipotence can do anything, in the latest as in the earliest ages.

Cheiromancy, Crystal-gazing, Astrology, and such like, are popular because they *are* superstitions: they have nothing to do with God; and they attribute effects to causes that have no existence as such. Nor are they popular because they are capable of a scientific explanation. If any scientific explanation were forthcoming they would lose popularity instead of gaining it. A cheiromantist who confined himself to saying that a man's character is expressed in his hand, as it is in his face, would have few devotees: he makes his money by pretending to read the future of his devotee in the lines if his palm. Crystal-gazing is believed in by those who in it imagine something inexplicable by reason; that belief in it is contrary to reason, loses it no adepts and no devotees. Astrology is not less admired because science declares that the Constellations have, and can have, no influence on the character or destiny of men.

Those who are too modern to believe in the archaism of such miracles as the Church declares to be possible, are delighted to believe in what science and reason alike declare to be impossible, because the former imply unchanging Omnipotence, to which all creation is subject, and the latter implies the existence of blind forces, helpless themselves, but potent to ruin the happiness and innocence of men.

OF MAJORITIES

OF all stupid vulgarities and sycophancies none, as it seems to me, is much more stupid, vulgar, and sycophantic than the abject prostration of the present age before majorities as such. If different ages, as has always been assumed, have had their special virtues and their special vices, there seems no reason why they should not also have their special vulgarities.

There may have been times when society abased itself before the thrones on which tyrants sat: but perhaps prostration was then mainly practised by courtiers, and they may have had the excuse of believing that they could not help themselves: to flatter Nero, Caligula, or Caracalla may have seemed to their unhappy servants but a venial condescension to sheer necessity, since they largely did it in the desperate hope of saving themselves from death and torture. And in some instances there is a healthy suggestion of irony in the compliments addressed to omnipotent ill-temper, as when the Chaldeans cried to the Babylonian tyrant, "O King, live for ever!" which happened to be the one thing which he could not do, as they knew, and he knew that they knew.

In later ages, when the thirst of certain nations

for liberty had clipped royalty of many of its prerogatives, the privileges of monarchs were commonly assumed to be in commission, and great Whig lords put on the halo of which they had stripped their masters. Flatteries as fulsome as any ever offered to Emperors and Kings were lavished on glorious beings who wore only coronets. The flatterers could not now allege fear and necessity, but they mostly did it for what they hoped to get out of it. Patronage was held tight in the fists of these guardians of the liberties of England: and those who flattered need not have been blind, but merely alive to the advantages of pensions and places. They set, however, a fashion, and it was followed, as fashions are, by many who had not anything definite to make by it: anybody powerful enough to start a mode, but unluckily short of one eye, may set a fashion of wearing the hair so as to conceal the empty orbit: of the thousands who follow it all but a few must be depriving themselves of half their vision. So arose that national characteristic of snobbery out of which one of the greatest of our writers has made a literature. But the *Book of Snobs,* though immortal, is obsolete or nearly: if Thackery were here to-day, and inclined to risk a sequel, it would not concern itself much with lords and their meek adorers—"faint but pursuing." No one would now think a celestial paradise attained by walking down Piccadilly arm-in-arm with two lords: a snobbish Duke would merely long to stroll through Limehouse with a local voter linked to each elbow. Of course there is the cult of wealth—apart from the greed of possessing it. The worship is, no doubt, of ancient prescription; but its liturgy, as enshrined in the Canon of the daily Press, is more fulsome, more abject, more shameless, and more cynical than it ever was before. That is one reason why the taste for high poetry and for high romance is almost extinct: the Golden Calf is the most arid theme for poets and romanticists; sapless of all inspiration, it is ignored by all inspired singing and all romance gilt with the light that never was on sea or land. A Press that grovels and slavers before millions of sovereigns is incomparably meaner than the trembling flatterer of an omnipotently cruel sovereign before whom he bowed simply to save his life. And the same Press that chaunts the Apotheosis of brutal wealth is as ready to proclaim the Infallibility of equally brutal majorities.

In both cases the ugly cult proceeds from the same cause. There is an instinct in the human animal for omnipotence: and God-given instincts, forbidden to tend whither they were meant, lie open to perversions the reverse of Divine. Thus men, taught to disbelieve in the immortality of the soul, reach out ever more wistful fingers after some substitute, as for the immortality of names and deeds: and even the outcast and the criminal will strive to snatch from the prurient curiosity of the only world they know an immortality of ignominy. And the modern Press helps them, as they know it will.

In the same way the modern confusion of masses of population that we are to call Society has decided to eliminate the idea of Divine omnipotence: if the idea persists it must be as a private idea, an idiosyncracy (and heavily taxable) : there is to be no public recognition of it: and yet there is the innate longing for omnipotence, somewhere, somehow. So the omnipotence of wealth is cajoled by people who are more impatient of poverty than any ever were till now, who *think* shame of poverty, and *cry* shame on riches, and, with greedy hands outstreched to snatch and steal them, proclaim them the accursed thing —the god-devil, adoring it with horrible abuse and envy, with self-tortures, agonised leapings towards it, and shrieking efforts to tear the golden idol down and share it piecemeal.

And the windy, empty hearts that have exiled Divine omnipotence profess to find its heir in the incoherent will of majorities.

This new flattery is as mean as the old: it is still the prostration of those who know that they know better, to a tyrant: still frightened, cowardly, abject. Only the tyrant has many heads, and millions of discordant tongues, unanimous never, except in the demand for destruction; sympathetic (even with itself), never, except in the irritable clamour for something new, for the trying of some rare and fatuous experiment; and ingenious never, except in devising plans for the sapping of foundations no matter what world-old fences and venerable edifices rest upon them. Until *"Pereat"* and *"Fiat"* mean the same thing *Vox Populi* and *Vox Dei* will never be synonymous.

But it is assumed that they are the same thing: or rather it is assumed that *Vox Dei* is a delusion, because it is assumed that Revelation never was *Vox Dei,* and never was more than the bleating of priests announcing their own inventions from behind a veil in a darkened sanctuary.

Just as every age has its peculiarly out-standing virtues, vices, and vulgarities, so may it have its distinctive superstitions. And the special superstition of this age of ours is the divinity ascribed to majorities—i. e., to brute numbers. It is based on the mathematical principle that by multiplying nothing by millions you get everything. The word of one foolish person is admittedly silly; but by adding to his voice those of a million others as silly as himself, the expression of infallible wisdom results. Each unit in the mob may be brutally ignorant, cruel, selfish, greedy, material, but the sum total of it all must be divine.

This superstition had to wait till faith had receded from the ground it was to occupy: and it can never seem very alluring to those who hold the Catholic faith in Christ. Where was the majority on Calvary? Which side did it take? What was it about? Have the majorities *ever* been on God's side since the fall of man? Was it to reward the fidelity of the mass of mankind that the deluge came? Were the prophets in the majority or those who stoned them? Has the whole world ever ranged itself on the side of the Church—does it now?

OF YOUTH AND EMOTION

IT may no longer be the fashion for elderly persons to warn the young against allowing themselves to be influenced by emotion and to preach up the glories of common sense. It certainly was the way when the present writer was young himself. It seemed, then, to be an axiom of the wise, i. e., of those who had turned forty, that "feeling," emotion, was dangerous, and an almost sure guide to disaster. Humble juniors succumbed to the theory; and, when they felt anything very strongly, knew that it behoved them to conceal the fact till they could cure it, else they would be belaboured with that tedious axiom. Emotion was assumed to be a phase of imprudence, its seed or embryo.

It was also insinuated that emotion was a weakness incident to youth, that should be outgrown as rapidly and completely as possible; to *have* outgrown it was one of the splendours of middle-age. It was, in fact, put in the corner, as a youthful delinquency.

No doubt there are vices of youth, and some of them bear fruit, with seasonable regularity and persistence, long after youth has gone for ever. Youth is sometimes selfish, but seldom so selfish as middle-age: what was a mere tendency at twenty is a deeply cherished habit at forty or fifty. Of course, we are to beware, in youth, the tendencies that will make our age abominable. But there are plenty of elderly vices that never were, so to speak, young: avarice, for instance, which, if ever seen in a boy, is seen so rarely that it almost makes a monster of its victim. Sloth, again, seldom disfigures a lad, though it does sometimes; but it is so common as hardly to seem a vice in elderly persons.

It is often taken for granted that youth is specially liable to irreligion, whereas it is only liable to a peculiar sort of thoughtlessness, that is apt to concern itself chiefly with the visible and obvious. If a census of this sort could be taken, I doubt if the majority of really irreligious people would be found among the young. A studious and self-conscious decorum has not much to do with religion. Youth is more given to speaking out than mature age, and all our transient irritations, likes and dislikes, will not sound religious when expressed. Middle-age is more cautious to express itself correctly, and has more experience as to what may be said without disapprobation: it has found the convenience of saying what other people say, and it mostly says it on every subject, whether it be art, literature, politics, ethics or religion.

And there is the speech of action: youth expresses itself, in this manner too, with a more disconcerting frankness than age. Like Adam before the fall, it is naked and not ashamed. Sometimes it acts like

Adam after the fall, and ought to be ashamed: but so does riper age; only riper age has learned to cover itself up. 'When it misbehaves it does not say so; rather the contrary.

I know it is the convention to talk as though the sins of sense were specially the sins of youth, and it is true that they are uglier and more disgusting in persons who are no longer young. But that they are really more common among young men than middle-aged men is assumed rather than proved. It is the grace of God that is our sanctuary from sin, not any point of life. Are the thoughts of the middle-aged and elderly, cleaner than those of youth? And a man's thoughts are often a truer picture of himself than anything he does: for no man ever yet rose above his highest thought, or fell beneath his lowest, and millions of men are lower than their external conduct, as many are really higher than sudden and isolated acts of theirs.

It is chiefly middle-age that insists on youthful faults: if youth retaliated it might have as much to say of the mean and sordid soul-smothering vices of age: but youth is mainly otherwise employed, and it has not envy to egg it on. What is there in middle-age for youth to be jealous of? What would not age give to be young again? So age, like the fox who had lost his tail, is at pains to preach its own superiority—at more pains, for that tail of youth can never, by any luck or solicitude, be made to grow again. Even preachers, I think, fall into the taint of this convention: many are young enough, but, instead of letting out their youth in sermons, they mostly assume a brevet of age, and preach as though they were in the decline of life. Elderly folk are assumed to be the only listeners, except when children are being specially preached to, and I can answer for one child who used to be peculiarly bored by children's sermons. Only very old priests, and children themselves, know how to preach to children: young men never can, but they could preach to young men if they would.

The elderly, having mostly lost that tail of emotion, are in a conspiracy to declare its danger. They do not discriminate much; nor is that surprising; it is not surprising that a Quaker should denounce any particular war, since he holds all war intrinsically evil; and those who have lost the capacity of all emotion can hardly distinguish between one and another. I do not count delight in a profitable investment among emotions, nor the transports of a Lord Mayor over a long over-due Baronetcy; those are sensations almost physical in their character.

Of course, there are people who are never middle-aged: in generous youth they linger on till the Great Hope dawns and makes them children again, not lately born, but on the exultant verge of birth. It is not they who decry emotion: it is what has kept their youth untarnished. And they know how few emotions that are real at all can be enkindled by what is of less than eternal significance. If emotion be, indeed, a special sign of youth it is because youth is nearer to the Eternity whence it was "struck out

as a spark, into the organised glory of things, from
the deep of the dark." They know that the much-
vaunted superiority to emotion is only the final
wearing-out of those clouds of glory we trailed with
us whence we came: the discarding of our intimations
of immortality: a common devolution, mean and sordid, nothing to brag of, but our cowardly compromise with imperfection and our truckling to it, our ab-
dication of ourselves as we might have been, our
resignation of the crown we might have worn over
ourselves, and our recognition that the mastery in
ourselves is to belong to the jostling majority of
unideal, utilitarian selfishnesses and greedinesses.

OF EMOTION AND COMMON SENSE

THOSE who cry down in the young that liability to Emotion which they have themselves outgrown, are seldom at pains to distinguish: it saves trouble to talk as if all Emotion were pretty sure to be worthless. And yet their own emancipation from it is not in general a proof of their being nearer heaven than they were in the far-away days when they too felt themselves uplifted on its airy wings; but rather a symptom of the world's influence, for worldliness and emotion are sworn enemies. That which the Eighteenth Century called Enthusiasm was near akin in spirit to Emotion: and when the Eighteenth Century spoke of enthusiasm it usually meant the attitude towards religion which is most disliked: a kind of polite chill was alone held to be safe and circumspect. The Evangelical revival and the Oxford Movement were equally revolts against the flat and worldly spirit admired by the dull Theism of the Eighteenth Century; and, divergent as their course was, each had its origin in, and derived its force from, the Enthusiasm abhorred by that very elderly century. Emotion in religion was assumed to be the very label of misguidedness: for religion, it was held, should consist in a detached concession to certain moral

apothegms, in which feeling had no share at all.
That the moral apothegms had been mostly
sanctioned by enlightened paganism, and implied
little that paganism would not have admitted, made
them seem all the more respectable to a century
that loved heathen Rome as much as it detested
Christian Rome.   The Pope is the arch-expression
of Christian Rome, and the Pope's arch-offence was
in his claim to be the Vicar of Christ; for the very
title of Vicar of Christ must always keep alive the
idea of a Personal God, and of a personal religion
expressing the intimate relations of every person
with God.   Whereas the religion of the admired
heathen was not a personal affair, and left the
feelings, that is, the heart, untouched: it came to
consist in a merely public admission of some ethical
truths that every State must profess in self-defence,
of a coldly theoretic morality which the admired
heathen had long ceased to apply to private
conduct.

Christian Rome stood for a personal relation
of every soul with Christ, which implied a sort of
interference highly objectionable to a society
formed by Voltaire, however it might profess some
mild regret at his excesses.   The "Grand Gibbon"
—his adjective, not ours—was the complete embodi-
ment of this attitude towards "Enthusiasm:" which
he abhorred because he thoroughly disliked
Christianity.   Enthusiasm is often no more than the
abiding result of Emotion: a large crop from its
little seed.

Instead of scolding down emotion, therefore, it would be more honest to distinguish. Of course there may be false emotion—but that is mere sentiment, and remarkably unlike true emotion and as different from it as prettiness is from beauty. And even true emotion may be transient and inoperative: but then the pity is, not that there was a brief dawn of emotion, but that the dawn came to no day: and many a true emotion, that was all on the side of the angels, was transient chiefly because it was frowned down, and stifled by the "prudent"—the prudent who are commonly supposed to be those indolent persons whose fear is always of doing too much: whereas what *has* been done has usually been done by them who tried to do much more, and might have done more but for them who were mortally afraid of doing anything—the Weaker Brethren, who never fail because they never attempt. The Weaker Brethren are not a prey to Emotion—nor was the Old Man of the Mountains; their office is the production of disagreeable sensations in others. It is very easy to take for granted, and very hard to prove, that Emotion is dangerous. I suspect it is, whenever genuine (and an insincere emotion is not readily conceivable) on the Angel's side. The Saints were glaring instances of Enthusiasm, and especially the Apostles: St. Peter was obviously subject to Emotion: and it did not prevent his Master choosing him for their Prince: perhaps it led him to his downward cross. St. Paul's letters pulse and throb with emotion—and

he is the villain of the piece of Christianity with
them who dislike it.

Common Sense is held up as the monitress of
Emotion: and the commoner it is, the more
complacently it submits to the role. Wisdom is
justified of her children, but Common Sense is only
her putative daughter, and has flat and vulgar
features that do not strongly bring to mind the
Wisdom of which the Holy Ghost tells us all. Till
Common Sense has learned to be a little less
worldly, her pose as an authority in spiritual matters
fits her ill. She is the goddess of worldly wisdom,
and to Christian ideas goddesses are unsympathetic.
Aware of this, she smugly poses as Prudence, and
assumes all the weight of a Cardinal Virtue; but the
real Christian Prudence, wary walker as she is, goes
undaunted with Charity's blazing torch to guide and
lead her: Common Sense prefers to sit down upon
it. The Saints had Christian Prudence in an
eminent degree, else they would never have been
canonized, but their Prudence showed itself in
making less of this world than of the next. That is
not at all the way with Common Sense. Her voice is
that of the current majority, extremely audible now
and here, and well enough content to drown a still,
small voice of which we have heard. "You had
better not," is her counsel of perfection. "Not"
and "better" are her synonyms. "Yes" and "Best"
are the synonyms of cardinal virtue Prudence.
"Come," says she to Emotion, "and I will show you
how to do it." "Go back," says Common Sense,

"and presently I will make you understand the cost of it all, the trouble of it, and the distance of the goal, how steep the way, and how stony, the brambles that shall scratch you, and the gibes that shall accompany you. The Kingdom of Heaven is *not* set upon a hill; Violence shall never take it by force: Violence is not particularly well-bred. Singularity is vulgar, and singularity consists in supposing you should try and do what everybody else is not doing already. Come, now, let me quench that flax of yours that only smokes, and enlightens no one, and warms no one: it makes our eyes smart and prevents your seeing what we all see—the exaggerated nature of your aims; nothing is so delusive as exaggeration."

As if the Devil never exaggerated, as if he never made inaccessible mountains out of trumpery mole-hills that honest effort could kick into dust. Of course the Devil never exaggerated the difficulties of decency and made people scoundrels out of despair, or kept middling Christians hovering at Heaven's gate out of a timorous shrinking from the excesses of perfection.

PSALMS OR "POORER STUFF"

THE Lenten Pastoral of one of our most gifted Bishops is a plea for the wider and more habitual use of the Psalter by the faithful in their prayers. He quotes St. Jerome to remind us of a time when the psalms were not treated as the monopoly of lettered clerks and cloistered monks or nuns, but were sung in every Christian home and by humble peasants at their toil, by the ploughman as he traced the slow furrow, by the vine-dresser as he pruned the vine, by lonely shepherds, and by the labourer as he wielded his heavy tools. The Bishop calls St. Chrysostom to witness how many that in his day had no literature, knew by heart the eternal songs of the poet-king.

For centuries after St. Jerome and St. Chrysostom, the Bishop notes, the Psalter was "the one prayer-book of all who could then read." "They have nourished the life of the Church in every age, and moulded the hearts of her saints." All who read the lives of the Saints must remember how spontaneously the words of the psalms arose to their lips in joy and sorrow, trial and jubilant thanksgiving. And, then, in a noble passage we are briefly shown how perfectly every phase of human emotion, every need of man's soul, every aspiration

85

of his spirit in penitence or devout love and gratitude, finds itself expressed for us in words that pass
our own powers but become at once our own, because they are God-inspired, and eternally true for
each of us, in these never-failing outpourings of one
of the greatest hearts that God ever made.

This world-poet sang not only for himself, but
of all things that in their infinite variety time cannot
wither nor custom stale—of God and all man; of
God alone; of the triple drama of Creation, Fall
and Redemption; of the Church, unborn yet, but to
be born out of the wounded side of Christ; of all
God's lovely world, Nature, as we call it, and the
universe of stars, the ring upon His creating finger,
the gems wherewith the fringe of His raiment is
jewelled.

In an ugly age we long for beauty, in a tired season we turn hither and thither for rest; and in the
psalms we find both as we can scarce find them elsewhere. Not that they are sad. The sorrowful
may in them find a sympathy that is incomparably
human because it is also divine; but they are often
exultant, often jubilant, a rhapsody of clear triumph
and delight as poignant as the skylark's. They are
more human than any other poems, and more spiritual. There is no instinct of man's more innate than
the relic of paradise that assails him with the desire
to rise above himself whither he came; and nowhere
is that instinct voiced with more wistful pathos than
in the psalms, nowhere more tenderly encouraged.

Who will give me wings like a dove,
And I will fly and be at rest.
Lo, far off have I gone, flying away,
And I abode in the wilderness. . . .

You shall be as the wings of a dove,
Covered with silver;
And the hinder parts of her back
With the paleness of gold.

One of the purest of our own poets knew that there are times when the loneliness of man will drive him far from men to find a salve for his wound in the wilderness where God is easier seen. It was no new discovery: the shepherd-king, who sang most sweetly of Him Who was to be King and Shepherd, had sung of it long before. Where is a Nature-song like this?

O Lord, my God, Thou art great, exceedingly!
Thou hast put on praise and beauty,
And art clothed with light as with a garment.
Who stretchest out, like a pavilion, the heavens:
Who coverest the higher rooms thereof with water:
Who makest the clouds Thy chariot:
Who walkest upon the wings of the winds:
Who makest Thine angels spirits
And Thy ministers a burning fire:
Who hast founded the earth on its own bases:
It shall not be moved for ever and ever:
The deep, like a garment, is its clothing.
Above the hills shall the waters stand . . .

Thou hast set a bound they shall not pass,
Nor turn again to cover the earth.
Thou sendest forth springs in the vales,
Between the midst of the hills shall the waters pass.
All the beasts of the field shall drink thereof,
And the wild asses wait in their thirst:
Over them the birds of the air shall dwell,
From out of the rocks shall they give forth their voices,
From Thy upper rooms Thou waterest the hills.
The earth shall be filled with the fruit of Thy works,
Bringing forth grass for cattle,
And herb for the service of men
That Thou mayest bring forth bread out of the earth
And wine that may cheer the heart of man.
The trees of the field shall be filled,
And the cedars of Libanus which He hath planted
There the sparrows shall make their nests—
The highest of them is the house of the heron;
The high hills are a refuge for the harts,
The rocks for the irchins.
He hath made the moon for seasons,
The sun knoweth his going down.
Thou hast appointed darkness,
And it is night;
In it all the beasts of the wood go about,
The young lions roaring after their prey
And seeking their meat from God.
The sun ariseth, and they are gathered together,
And they shall lie down in their dens.
Man shall go forth to his work
And to his labour till the evening.
How great are Thy works, O God!
Thou hast made all things in wisdom,
The earth is filled with Thy riches.

So is this great sea
Which stretcheth wide its arms.
There are creeping things without number,
Creatures little and great.
There shall the ships go,
And this sea-dragon
Which ·thou hast formed to play therein:
All wait for thee to give their food in season. . . .

But this book of universal poems is much neglected
now by those who choose their prayers for themselves. ". . . and if to-day they seem to be ousted
from their place of honour, and to have made room
for poorer stuff, this does but show that many, in
selecting their devotions, prefer the compositions
of men and women, albeit pious, to those of the
Source of Holiness itself."
The Church leaves each of us free to choose
among the Saints those whom each prefers for
special patrons; nevertheless, she shows that among
the Saints are some who must receive the devotion
of us all, as Christ's Mother and St. Peter. Nor
does she fussily dictate uniformity in private prayer
to those who, holding one faith, belong to every
clime and age; to young and old, to northern and
southern, to lettered and unlettered, to the coarse
and the refined—for the coarse and vulgar may be
saved too. Yet by her own example she hints at
what would be best for all; and into the hands of
all on whom she lays the *obligation* of stated prayer
she puts the psalms: the prayer of the priest and of
the religious, as she enjoins it on them, consists, as to

nine parts out of ten, of psalms. And these, her
clergy and her religious, are her salt wherewith the
whole soil of her kingdom is to be seasoned. From
them, therefore, she looks for a piety the most
sincere, the most virile, the most practical and
genuine; and to form it, and feed it, to give it its
character and colour, its sinews and its nerves, she
puts into their praying mouths the psalms. The
most loyal and loving child obeys without a word of
command, on the first apprehension of his mother's
desire. And from what the Church does herself
we may teach ourselves what to do. When *she*
prays it is with the psalms.

But there is a piety barely skin-deep, exotic and
heat-forced, not much inured to sharp breeze or
nipping frost, not of the outdoor, work-a-day sort,
not over-masculine, nor vigorous, nor meant for
rough usage. And it likes prettiness better than
beauty, sentiment more than sense, rhetoric rather
than resolve; and the psalms are not much loved by
it. They hardly lend themselves to it—though they
lend themselves to all that is real, virile, and genuine. The psalms are divine prayer, and what this
sort of piety prefers is not even manly.

SELF AND SELF-SACRIFICE

IT is no grand discovery that war, whose ruin and pain all can perceive, may be a medicine of Omnipotence for surfeited peoples grown wanton in prosperity. That has always been known, and it is a thing we may need to remember, but are not now to learn: unless, indeed, we can be said to learn that which we have wilfully forgotten and are forced to call to mind.

Among the worst effects upon a person, or upon a people, that a long course of prosperity may produce, is that of selfishness, which is nothing else than an oblivion of the Two Great Commandments of the Law. The love of God, above all things, and the love of our neighbour as ourself, are ousted by the portentous self-consideration engendered by too great facilities for indulging it.

And security of ease in self-indulgence is apt to produce in a nation, which is only a many-headed (or many-stomached) person, what it tends to produce in an individual. So God, who cares more for our good than for our goods, intervenes: and we are reminded of things.

His commandments are only Divine sanctions of facts that we cannot ignore without ruining ourselves. In our petulance of youth, perhaps, we

wish, in our unavowed secret hearts, that He had
not made so many commandments: as if their
number had been arbitrary and casual, and there
might have been fewer had irresponsible Omnipotence so chosen.   But presently we perceive that,
if God had been silent, man would have had to make
the Commandments for himself.   That is our discovery about the Ten Commandments.

The Two Great Commandments of the Law are
more summary, and at first may strike us as less
intimate, a sort of transcendental generalisation
towards which we admit a nodding acquaintance, and
pass on not unwillingly.   And, if we do, we are
ruined again.   For they also are only a statement
of impregnable fact.   God matters to man more
than man matters to himself; and no individual man
can stand alone heedless of his fellow men.   God,
in the beginning, said: "It is not good for man
to be alone": because he cannot; if he tries, he
becomes a monster, nor less horrible to angels
because he may be, by a whole civilisation, removed
from a savage; to angelic loyalty, and to angelic
intelligence, indeed, that which we call civilisation
may not appear peculiarly beautiful.   There was
only one perplexing rebellion in heaven: to the un-
fallen angels loyalty is the only beauty, and terres-
trial civilisation has often been disloyal to Heaven's
King and ours.   To celestial intelligence mundane
efforts to find happiness and freedom without God
can only appear perverse stupidity: a pitiable

attempt to make emptiness look full and rottenness smell sweet.

Still, the attempt is made: each new civilisation tries the experiment. God, it asserts, in more or less decorous phrase, civic or national, is not essential to it: and each individual man proceeds to feel: "Neither is anyone else to me."

And, because God's facts are facts for all men and for all time, then come the barbarians and blow up the civilisation that had two mines under it. Now war, itself very often the direct consequence and ripe fruit of a monarch's or a nation's selfishness, serves often for the sharp and searching medicine against these two poisons of forgetfulness. While it rigorously reminds us of undethroned Omnipotence, and sends us piteously entreating to the steps of that throne, it also brings us back to the sense that isolation in ourselves will not do. A common danger and a common dread compel us to remember our need of others, and their need of us; and we perceive that this need is greater and more real than our need of mere things; forced to recognise Death's august and dread presence in our midst, at our threshold, we no longer can think life less than the trappings of it.

And this awakening to a poignant mutual need and inter-dependence between us and our brothers sets alight a generosity by whose warmth our self-absorption is kindled to self-sacrifice.

We may see that happening all over England to-day and all over the great family of peoples that is called by the name of British Empire. But what happens closest to our own eyes is what we most plainly notice.

Here, then, we witness a great and significant change in the attitude and demeanour of the people. It is more grave; and everywhere there is a marked disposition to share in the common work and the common self-denial. A noble example of this disposition of heart and mind is that given by them who have enlisted for military or naval service since the war began. It is a thing that cannot now be done lightly: and it is done with the deliberate purpose of going to help, or to relieve, them who have borne the first terrific onslaught of the enemy: out of a high and noble determination that *they* shall not be left unaided, that on *them* shall not fall the whole burden and the whole danger.

But a short while since and no young man became a soldier except to please himself: that is no longer the idea: immense numbers of those who have now taken service, whether as officer or as private soldier, have done so against all, every inclination of mere taste and liking. They are young men, who if it were time of peace, would never have turned, by choice, to the profession of arms. They are, many of them, undergraduates of great universities, whose imagined careers were to have been wholly different: numbers of others have left posts of comfort and emolument, not too easy to have gained, which they were filling to their own satisfaction and that of their employers. Nothing is more striking than the way in which men, and mere lads, too, of the highest and of the upper and lower middle-classes, have laid aside their own pleasures and profit, and that very largely out of the simple motive of not leaving to comrades already in the field, comrades bound to it by previous engagement, the given dangers and sufferings of a calling which they themselves had never meant to follow, which they never chose when it involved neither suffering nor danger. And what is true of the young men of those classes is true of the young men of a lower class who have recently enlisted and are enlisting now. It is no fancy for a red coat that has called them from their homes, from the fields whose ridges have been their horizon, from their factories and their workshops: theirs is no red coat. To them the soldier life, untried and unknown, is strange and mostly uninviting. They also have much to sacrifice —everything that they know and are used to: and they, too, have but one life apiece, and most, in leaving home and the friends they have cared for, take it in their hands whither they barely know and whence there may be no return. And this heroic, plain thing they are brought to do most of all lest they should seem to be leaving in the lurch men not yet their comrades: because they will not sit selfishly by a secure hearth while those others bear and are in danger.

There are a thousand arguments against a voluntary army: there may arise an absolute neces-

sity to lay aside its principle to save the life of our
nation: but in the meantime it has this singular and
splendid quality, that every soldier offering himself
to it at a juncture like the present is doing what I
have tried to describe.   And hundreds of thousands
have done it, and are doing it, up and down the
country.

Each man, I say, who so acts is the centre of a
self-sacrifice that extends far beyond himself.   In
so abdicating himself and his own selfish likings he
mounts, however silently and humbly, a throne from
whose steps selfishness shrinks away out of sight,
and to which innumerable acts and impulses of self-
sacrifice crowd as courtiers.   He infects—'tis an
old pleasure of mine to insist how good and noble
conduct and ideas are just as infecting as bad and
mean—he infects a whole neighbourhood: and the
mere movements of natural affection set going
springs of generosity and self-sacrifice: fathers,
mothers, sisters, friends, who cannot soldier, must
do what they can for the lad who has chosen that
hard and noble part at such a time as this.   You see
it in operation all over the Empire, in every class
and condition of life: though it never may be known,
here on earth, *what* has been done, is being done, by
the rich and by the poor, and by those, perhaps,
whose self-denial costs most of all, the poor who are
forced by tyrannous but not ignoble convention to
seem to belong rather to the rich than to the poor,
who may not go ragged, who must uphold the

slowly-dying tradition of a gentle name and gentle habits.

What, I wonder, have this past Christmas's presents to our troops and to our ships cost all these? What pinchings at home? What laying aside of little pleasures and luxuries grown almost sacred by custom and association?

A Merry Christmas! Who durst use that beloved phrase—coming down to us from days when Merry meant, in English, a word that might be fitted to angelic Christmas in Heaven—who, I say, durst use it this time? Whatever motto was on the cards, the real one, unwritten, was self-sacrifice.

THE GOLDEN ROAD

FOR the first time for forty years I passed, in the train last week, the station where I used to get out when going to my first school: and presently the boys will be hurrying down there from the many-spired town to go home for Christmas. I call them all my school-fellows, just as when I was there (with their grand-fathers, perhaps). I thought of Addison and David Garrick, of Dr. Johnson and Elias Ashmole as my school-fellows . . . and will the journey home seem to them as it used to seem to me in those far-away days that crowd closer on me, and have a more intimate nearness than the summers of these years since I have grown old? I hope so; for it seemed a golden journey, not like any others, half unearthly, and yet the most perfectly homely of any one could make—homewards, and for Christmas. The gold was not in my pocket—of that sort of gold there was little at home, either: to buy my ticket I needed one bit, and the change left was not abundant; but it did not matter in the least: of course, there were millions of things one could have bought, but to go without them was no hardship; the thought of them was possession enough, and kept alive a wider sense of rich possibilities than prosaic acquisition could have yielded. I never remember envying rich people, least of all other boys, who might be rich: the richness of the wealthy was part of the world (that belonged to me, too), and varied it, as lovely parks and old castles do, making it more interesting for me: England would have been a much duller place for one and everybody if it were clipped out in allotments of a mediocre prosperousness. Even the shops would have suffered, for they would never have been so well worth looking at if they had held only the sort of things I could ever have pictured myself able to buy. Rich boys I certainly could not be jealous of, for the richest of them had not *my* home, and I would not have given sixpence for anybody else's. And I was going there—

That was why the cab that rattled and rumbled me down to the station, and was dampish, and had a smell like a cold stable, never aroused in me the slightest adverse criticism: the lean velveteen or corduroy padding, the jolts and creaks, the clattering windows, were merely a part of the general sublime episode—home-going. The horse had broken his knees so often that he was pretty indifferent to breaking them again; the driver might cock his hat with a forlorn attempt to look doggish and slightly dissipated, an attempt somewhat assisted by his holly-berry nose; but to me they were both friendly and cheerful creatures, bound to bring me to the train that would carry me to the place I had been hungry for, dying with hunger for, all these months. The horse always did go quick enough for that, and the cabman even forced him into a monstrous feint of galloping for the last hundred yards. That was to earn my modest tip, on which the man spat for luck, not scornfully at all as he wished me "a merry Christmas when it comes"—full well he knew that next time we should meet the sight of him would not be so pleasant. There were Christmas hampers in the station (not nearly so many as now) and bundles of mistletoe and evergreens; and the porters handled them with a friendly sympathy, or trundled them along on big barrows with little wheels, calling out, "By your leave!"—as if anyone would give leave to have his toes wheeled over! The man who sold you your ticket had a generous look, as though aware that it was worth double the money, but you were welcome to it—not like the fellow at our own station who would ask as much in five weeks for a very different ticket with a conscious air of monstrous imposition. Of *him* one did not choose to think. Your own particular porter (in a waistcoat with black calico sleeves: if Mr. Lloyd George alters *them*, then, indeed, will he have completed the destruction of that England I knew as a boy) came for *his* tip, too, not hintingly, but with calm reliance on the presence of justice in a world that even then was said (by elderly persons) to have its faults. He did not spit on the money, but rendered it invisible to mortal eye without seeming to pocket it, and certainly not holding it in his hands, as he clapped them together, saying it was seasonable weather and looked like snow.

"And a merry Christmas, sir, and a happy New Year, when it comes," he called out as the train began to move.

The trains went slower then, and took more cognizance of intermediate stations—at least, mine did, and I thought it an advantage: one saw more of one's native country and gathered a fuller realization that it was the journey home for Christmas, to which every stop, with all its one-tuned incidents, contributed, like the countless notes of a symphony, each valueless alone, but altogether making the wonderful sweet music.

These cold Midlands outside the windows would have given but a poor notion of England's beauty to a stranger; flat, raw fields under a low, grey sky, ragged hedgerows, broken by trees, naked, and not usually very big; but I knew how lovely are the quiet, plain things that go to make an English countryside when you can see them closely and leisurely, not glancing dully on them, as on a jumbled succession of maps. And all about were dotted homesteads and cottages, each a warm heart of life, all the tenderer for not flaunting it too publicly.

Through the level pastures crept a slowly-winding canal, continually reappearing when it seemed to have been left miles behind, with mellow, lichen-crusted bridges; and I liked it better, somehow, than a river, for in rivers only fishes have their homes. Canals carry on their unturbulent, still bosoms a never-ending procession of homes of men and women and their children, who are always moving (like all of us) and always at home, go where they will (as we all are, so long as it means to us our Father's rest and presence.)

I saw the slow barge-houses moving deliberately through the patient, winter lands, the long, long rope behind them, now taut, now oddly slack, though the boat never stopped, and at the end of the long barge, with its queer, delightful house and the father steering, outside his own front door. His children played upon the roof; his wife was hanging out her Christmas wash to dry on the lines that ran along a path of plank reaching from stem to stern. She was evidently joking with the little ones, and they were skipping and laughing, while their odd, mongrel terrier yapped at a passenger on the towing-path and made dashes at him that nearly sent his shaggy little body overboard. And the bargeman pretended to encourage his dog, and the wayfarer on the foot-path didn't mind, but laughed and holloed "A Merry Christmas!" The noisy, disreputable-looking cur meant no harm, and couldn't get at him if he did; and wasn't *he* going home for Christmas, too?—home, I was certain, to yonder grey-red mill on the little hill, where a mealy-looking man (the traveller's father, it was plain) was running out and calling to the stout, comfortable, elderly woman who came out at once, wiping soap-suds from her ruddy arms. And the traveller had a mistletoe-sprig in his cap, and the bargeman had a bit of holly in his, and over the roof tilted a pole

with intertwined hoops hanging from it, all wreathed
in ivy and holly and mistletoe.

Then came the change at the great junction, and
the wait there that I counted as half the day's ad-
ventures; the hurrying Christmas traffic, the book-
stall bristling with Christmas numbers of hollyish
outside, and robins, with snowy pictures, and never
a pretence that Christmas, after all, is a tiresome,
expensive season; and crowds of people going everywhere, but all going home to keep Christmas and
knit up ravelled threads of love and friendliness.
All strangers, and the more exciting; all unknown,
but all intimate friends bound to each other and to
me by the golden cord of Christ's near birthday,
and with one set purpose of keeping it together—
only seemingly apart. They have reached home
now, many, many of them; and so shall I soon; but
on the way they left a pleasant trail behind of smiles
and laughing; and many of their smiles fell kindly
on the stranger face of the boy they never saw before, and never would see again, but home-bound,
too—a fellow traveller. And so, without speaking,
they also gave him Merry Christmas, and he thanks
them for it yet.

After a good hour and a half of this ungrudged
waiting and watching of all those crossing currents
of the great life that was part of me, as I of it, a
train that seemed smaller, and was certainly slower,
took me on; no longer by the great main line north
and west, but by a cross country line, where no one

seemed to be going so far, and most of the passengers had a look of nearing their journey's end. One knew the names of all the stations now and the exact order in which they would be reached, and many of the people standing about the platforms had quite familiar faces, though unknown names.

Then another change and a shorter wait, at a much smaller junction, where you began to hear Welsh talked by the passengers—all the women were knitting and some of them wore the odd steeple-hats that even then were growing rare. After that there were only three or four stations, and first each hill and wood, and soon each tree in the windy hedgerows had a familiar, friendly look, and seemed to call out, Welcome Home.

The wintry day was closing in when the journey was ended—and who could be sorry? Our little streets looked warmer and more welcoming with the shops lighted up, and home itself never *could* look so dressed for welcome as when it shut itself close against the snow that was just beginning, but opened itself to fold you in.

Along that same Golden Road the passengers will now be hurrying, our Father's other children, our countless unknown brothers and sisters: and we must needs think of them, and pray Him bless their journey, and bring them also home.

CONTINUITY VERSUS IDENTITY

WHAT some very excellent people mean by Continuity they themselves must be supposed to know, though what it is they do mean not everyone else is capable of grasping: what Identity means even ordinary people are able to perceive with all practical correctness. I say with all practical correctness, because no one wants to pretend that perception necessarily implies the faculty of accurate definition. There may be a million persons, or more, who know perfectly what a tree is, for one who could define a tree scientifically. Perhaps a child's power of recognition, of perception of what any known object is, is as clear as that of the most cautious adult, but only phenomenal children have any faculty of exclusive definition. Probably ninety-nine children out of a hundred have as true an idea as their teachers of what a spirit is, but nine out of ten will say, if you ask them, that a spirit is something you can't see, without pausing to remember that you can't see the East Wind, or the smell of a halfpenny egg, and may not be able to see your own feet, though they can see theirs. We are not just now concerning ourselves either with children, who usually can define nothing, or with adults of trained thought and speech who are accustomed to define all their meanings with perfect accuracy. Ordinary adults do not belong to that class. For ordinary people mean a great deal more than they would ever take the trouble to define.

And ordinary people, without defining it, have a just and plain appreciation of what is implied in identity. When they talk of identifying a man they mean ascertaining, or proving that he is himself, and is not somebody else; and, on the whole, they have a sufficiently correct notion how it can be done. If the particular man in question is well known to themselves it would be very hard to convince them that some other person was he: astounding cases of personal resemblance occur, but they are phenomenal, and personal resemblance in such a case would not settle the matter: identity would not be admitted without a number of other proofs, and the offered proofs break down, for the straightforward and simple reason that the claimant is *not* the man he says, but another. This common notion of identity does not, even among the most ordinary people, preclude the idea of development, or (as they call it) "change." The Queen Victoria who celebrated her Diamond Jubilee had developed vastly from the Princess of 1837: she had "changed" immensely in those sixty years, as was inevitable, seeing that during all those three-score years she had been alive: she was, as we say, a different person; but none of her subjects doubted that she was the same person. Every sane man was certain of the "identity" of the old Queen with the maiden

Princess in spite of all the development and change, in spite of all anyone could say as to there being not one atom of her body, blood, or bone the same after sixty years as before, in spite of all conceivable change in opinion, colour of thought, like, dislike, or what not.

And ordinary people can and do recognise identity in other things than individual persons: for instance, they can and do perceive the identity with herself of the Catholic Church, no matter where they see her. Many of them dislike her extremely; and those who dislike her most, detest the sight of her equally in Ireland and Italy, Austria and Andalusia, Sicily and Sardinia, Chile and China, Portugal and Peru. No matter in what language Catholicity is expressed it is equally offensive to these persons, so long as they can understand it at all. Some Catholics may be well educated, or plausible, or (what is better) well-off, but their Catholicity is as intolerable as that of the most ignorant, the least adroit, and the poorest, because it *is* Catholicity, and all the same thing.

Without mentioning Catholics themselves, who like their own Church everywhere, there are many non-Catholics who respect the Church, and have good words for her. And they also fully recognise the identity of the Catholic Church with itself all over the world. It may be urged by some that Catholicity shows to more advantage in one country than in some other; an Ulster Protestant thinks it shows to peculiar disadvantage in Ireland; but the

likers and dislikers all feel that the Catholic Church
is one and the same.   If the Catholic Faith could
be regarded as a local or national idiosyncrasy it
would not be the bugbear it is to many persons.
Nor are her enemies merely our present contemporaries; she may have new enemies in a new age,
but she has had enemies a long while, and they
bear witness to her identity with herself all along.
In spite of all the development nineteen centuries
must imply in a living organism, her offensive
identity remains unmistakable and unpardonable.
She is the same villain of the piece through a tedious
sequence of ages.   Should some milder critic plead
that she has improved, these others would scout
the notion of any radical improvement—because she
is the same, in spite of any seeming changes incurably
one with herself always.   Should a sterner critic
scold her as worse now than ever, he would himself
admit that she had only done at last what she, in her
nature, in the inexorable logic of growth, was bound
to do sooner or later; that her present faults were
not accidental but inbred in her bone and sinew, her
heart, mind, and spirit, the inevitable result of her
being what she is, and always was, the honest yielding to her unchangeable, but living, character; the
throwing off of a mask, perhaps, but then that
process only reveals identity more clearly.

It is labouring a stale point, all this, no doubt, a
point that does not at all concern the vast majority of
non-Catholics, any more than it concerns us.   But it
does concern the wistful plea of Anglican continuity

with the pre-Reformation Church in England. The continuity plea demands ruthlessly one of two things: either the assertion that the Catholic Church, as understood not only by Catholics themselves but by non-Catholics of every sort, the schismatic Eastern Communions, the Protestant sects, the whole world of Islam, the vast body of Buddhist believers, and the huge agglomeration of non-believers —that the present Catholic Church, I say, is not, change or no change, development apart, the Catholic Church of the Middle Ages; which necessitates the further assertion that the Catholic Church has now ceased to exist; and that it did not, in the Middle Ages, exist in England. Or else a proof that the present Church of England is identical with the Catholic Church of Spain, Ireland, Italy, Austria, South America, and so on. Continuity implies identity. Let us presently consider (1) the non-existence of the Roman Church; (2) the identity of Anglicanism with the Roman Church, if it still exists.

Neither of these points concerns the bulk of mankind that has its mind made up on them; but both of them concern closely the dwellers in that shadowy realm where "continuity" is necessary to sustain life.

THE WIND AND THE SHORN LAMB

ONE cannot say everything at once: and it is to be remembered that, for our present purpose, there is no need to consider whether the Catholic Church, as she was known to the Christendom of the Middle Ages, had or had not diverged from "Primitive" Christianity. That, as Mr. Kipling used to say, is another story. It does not for the moment concern us to prove that, as the Church had been *alive* during all the centuries that joined the Middle Ages to the "Primitive Age," the alleged divergence amounted to no more than natural growth and the development of inherent principles. For the holders of "Anglican Continuity" do not in the least doubt that there was a Catholic Church in the Middle Ages; they do not deny, or wish to deny, that in the centuries immediately preceding the Reformation the Catholic Church existed; they are convinced she did exist in England, France, Italy, Spain, Germany, etc.,—in Christendom at large. The Catholic Church was the Church of all those countries; that the believers in "Continuity" fully admit and assume. Then came the Reformation, which they largely dislike; which we also dislike, but cannot ignore; they, on the other hand, are really disposed to ignore it; for while we perceive (as the unconcerned outside world clearly perceived, and has always known) that the Reformation changed the religion of England; they are driven, by their new plea of Continuity, to deny or ignore that change and to assert that what had been the religion of England under the Plantagenets remained the religion of England under the Tudors, Stuarts, and Hanoverians: that Cardinal Beaufort, who became Bishop of Winchester in 1405, and Dr. Benjamin Hoadly, who became Bishop of Winchester in 1734, were Bishops of the same Church. That Cardinals Langton, Kilwarly, Langham, Stafford, Kemp, Bourchier, Morton and Pole not only held the See of Canterbury before Dr. Tillotson —of whom the Benchers of Lincoln's Inn complained that "since Mr. Tillotson came Jesus Christ has not been preached among us"—but were Bishops of the same Church as that to which Tillotson belonged.

If, however, the Church to which Hoadly and Tillotson belonged was the Catholic Church, then the Catholic Church existed in England only, and had ceased to exist anywhere else. For no one except the continuity folk, Catholic or Calvinist, Jew or Turk, can believe that Cardinals, of any country, contemporary with Hoadly and Tillotson, belonged to the Church of which those gentlemen were ornaments.

Apparently the Reformation had an effect even more damaging than any even *we* attribute to it; for, while it left England in possession of the Catholic

Church and Faith, it destroyed the Catholic Church and Faith everywhere else!

England which discarded the Pope, and five sacraments, and discarded Purgatory, the invocation of saints, the sacrifice of the Mass, monks, nuns, and a great deal besides, remained Catholic. Rome, and all who continued in her obedience, retained all those things, just as they had been held in the times of all Cardinals, Archbishops of Canterbury or York, Bishops of Winchester, Lincoln, Rochester, Salisbury, Durham, and so on, but ceased to be Catholic.

Providential for England? Yes, but (as Dickens would say) a little particular of Providence. It was perhaps, hard on that vastly larger part of Christendom that hadn't changed its beliefs at all to have lost the Faith altogether; while the little bit that had thrown its ancient beliefs overboard was left in solitary possession of the real Catholic Faith! Hard, that, except in England, the real Catholic Faith had expired at the Reformation.

Of course, a blow is never so painful when one is wholly unconscious of it; a pain that you don't feel doesn't hurt so much, and foreign Christendom was quite unaware that it had lost its Catholic Church and Faith. Italy, France, Spain, Austria, Hungary, Ireland, Poland, half Germany, and so forth, had not the least idea that they had become mere "Romans," while in happy England nothing particular had happened, in spite of delusive appearances to the contrary. They did not realise that in holding what their forefathers had held they had fallen from the Faith, while the true believers were those who, lonely in the northern sea, had discarded those veteran beliefs and held whatever they chose, so long as it was *not* what their forefathers had believed. The bishops of Italy, France, Spain, Poland, Ireland, Austria, Hungary and unreformed Germany went on obeying the Pope, just as the unreformed bishops in England had done, without ever awakening to the fact that true ecclesiastical obedience lay in contradiction, vilification, and defiance; and their simple flocks followed them. Monks and nuns abroad went on keeping the same rule that had been kept in England for a thousand years without adverting to the fact that in the insular, but true, Catholic Church monasticism was abolished. People abroad adored the veiled Christ of the Eucharist without realising that they should wait for several centuries till the results of the Oxford Movement should have legitimised the practice: they went openly to confession to a priest, and had Masses said for their dead friends, and begged our Lady and the Saints to pray for them— all without perceiving that such small matters were in abeyance for the next three centuries or so: in fact, they went on, up and down Europe, just as if nothing had happened to *them*, and the disaster had fallen on the English. Shorn of their Catholicity, these foreign lambs had the bleak wind of their loss tempered to them by being simply unaware of it. What had happened to them was unknown, not only to them, but to all the world beside, except in

England—and England kept the secret for several centuries: it was not till the nineteenth century that anyone even in England spoke up, and let it be known that the Reformation had *not* cut England free from the Catholic Church: that the Reformation Church of England had remained Catholic (obviously without suspecting it for a few ages): that Dr. and Mr. Parker had belonged to the same Church as Cardinal Pole; and Dr. and Mr. Hoadly to the same Church as Cardinal Beaufort—but that Cardinal Wiseman, Cardinal Newman, Cardinal Manning, and Cardinal Vaughan did *not* belong to the same Church as Cardinal Langton, Cardinal Bainbridge, or Cardinal Morton: for no one ever doubted the Catholicity of those ancient Cardinals, or called them "Romans" (though princes of the Roman Church and eligible, each of them, to the papacy itself). This singular result, it was discovered, had been produced on the Catholic Church by a Protestant Reformation—or at the time when a Protestant Reformation was commonly believed to have occurred, but hadn't really—that whereas, before it, all English Bishops and Cardinals in communion with Rome had been Catholic, after it all English bishops in communion with Rome were not Catholic but schismatic: that those who had never dropped one iota of Catholic belief were Catholic no longer, and those who had abjured nearly every distinctively Catholic dogma were Catholic still. Certainly it was a comfort to these faithful schismatics that the wind of their bleak schism, involving the great majority of ecclesiastical Christians, was tempered to them by ignorance of their unhappy state: and it was odd that no strangers suspected what had happened to them. Jews in Rome, Paris, Vienna, Toledo, Warsaw, Munich, Brussels, and so on, were quite in the dark as to the great fact that what had been the Catholicity of their neighbours had become schismatic, since all these "Roman Catholics" belonged to the same Church with the Roman Catholics of Dublin or London, whose Church was no longer Catholic but schismatic.

The Lutherans of Northern Germany and Scandinavia, the Calvinists of Switzerland, the Presbyterians of Scotland, the Huguenots of France, and the English Nonconformists supposed that men like Cardinal Beaton, Cardinal Mazarin, the Cardinal Duke of York, Cardinal Allen, Cardinal Cullen, and so on, all belonged to one and the same Church, the old Church to which Langton, Wolsey, Beaufort, or Bainbridge had belonged, which their incomparable Reformation had driven out of Scandinavia and Scotland, England, and half of Switzerland, Holland and half Germany: and they had not the least idea that the Reformation had done no such thing in England, but that the old Catholic Church flourished as ever in England under their Graces of Canterbury and York, with merely a Hanoverian Pope not in holy orders.

And so of the Gallios, who troubled themselves not at all with such matters: did Frederick the Great ever know that the State Church of England was the

ancient Catholic Church of that country? Did
Voltaire? Did Napoleon? We know that George
Washington never told a lie; would he have been
ready to affirm that the Church of which George III.
was the legal head was the identical Church of which
Adrian IV. had been the head, undoubtedly Catholic
then?

When Henry IV. of France turned Catholic did
Queen Elizabeth think he had joined the religion of
her bishops? She didn't seem to think much of her
bishops: was that why it annoyed her?

"Oh, Liberty!" cried Madame Roland, "the
things that are done in thy name!"

"Oh, Continuity!" we must exclaim, "the things
that would have to be said for thy sake!"

CONTINUITY AND CARDINALS

"SIXPENCE in the box, please, for each visitor—thank you, sir," said the verger; and, being satisfied (the box having a glass front) that a shilling had gone down, he threw open the iron gate giving access to the south aisle of the choir, and bowed two visitors in. "The one with the puce tie (or shirt-front; would it be a shirt-front?)," he perhaps informed himself, as he resumed his seat by the box with the glass front, "is some sort of Catholic priest."

The other, who was not elderly, might be anything. "Just a lame 'un." The two visitors passed on, wondering how long it would take, at the present apparent rate of progress, to fill in the whole walls of the Cathedral with glittering brass panels. Having admired William of Wykeham's noble chantry in the nave, they were somewhat impatient to reach the other chantry-tombs in the "retro-choir," and hardly willing to do more than pause a moment by the exuberant monument of Bishop Wilberforce in the transept.

"Soapy Sam!" one of them murmured, not ungratefully, mindful of some of the courtly prelate's classic witticisms. Then, since the six stone angels in charge can say nothing, he offered a little prayer, and turned to the steep steps. There was another tomb to pray by, much less ornate, in mid-choir, where for centuries it has lain before the great altar, through thousands of Requiems and Dirges, low, plain, and sombre, with no courtly phrases of epitaph —the Red King's. Though all these requiems and dirges of over four hundred years had been for him, he would need them all, if ever he were to see that Face he would swear by so hardily. What could a stranger do but stand by the low dark stone and offer them all up again, as though in truth they had been meant for him whose mad heart had crumbled to dust within? It was strange to think that had he been some great servant of God, instead of His rebel, these dry bones might long ago have been torn hence and scattered to the winds.

It was strange, too, to look up at the countless carven figures of the huge reredos, not all original and ancient: to see the sculptured bishops, in mitre and chasuble, dalmatics and alb, gloves and buskins, as the bishops of Rome's obedience wear them to-day: and, midmost of all, to see the great stone crucifix, and remember its perfect legality, being a wall-fixture, and how illegal and affronting it would be if it stood, where stands the empty cross, on the shelf beneath.

The younger visitor was venerating, not super-stitiously, but genealogically and eclectically, the regal bones, Saxon and Danish, hidden in coffers high up on the stone screen: for some were his ancestors, and some were not. And so, presently,

the two visitors left the choir and came to the grove
of tombs and chantries behind: Richard Fox's,
Stephen Gardiner's, William of Waynflete's,
William of Edindon's: three of them Chancellors
of England, one of them Lord Privy Seal—and all
of them *such* Protestants! How plainly had their
lives and deeds shown them members of the same
Church with their successor down yonder in the
transept, my lord Samuel of quippish memory!

But of all those tombs and chantries the most
significant there is Beaufort's. One stands a few
paces off; behind perhaps, with the plain eastern
side of the great reredos at one's back, and the
southern sun shines in and lights up the massive
painted figure on the tomb: the red robes and red
hat give out all their colours in the caressing light.
One may have just come from St. Cross, which he
refounded; which stands still among the green meads
by the river, a lovely monument of princely, and
better than princely generosity and tenderness for
the old and broken, as the College hard by is of
Wykeham's reverent love of youth, and that other
loveliest college, by that other river, is of Waynflete's: but thick as these memories of good deeds
crowd, they are not the point that hits and insists,
and urges itself here.

Yonder Winchester Bishop, lying there in Rome's
scarlet, might be no effigy, but a figure just dead,
lying by Peter's tomb, in Peter's basilica, for
reverence before his burial: a dead Cardinal. He
was a Cardinal: like his predecessor, the first founder

of St. Cross; like Langton of Canterbury, and Kil-
warby, and Langham, Stafford, Kemp, and Bour-
chier, Morton, Warham and Pole, all Primates of
England; like Thoresby, Kemp, and Bainbridge, of
the Northern Primacy; like Louis de Luxemburgh,
Bishop of Ely; Philip de Repingdon, Bishop of
Lincoln; Pandulph, Bishop of Norwich; John
Fisher, Bishop of Rochester; Robert Hallum,
Bishop of Salisbury; John Thoresby, Bishop of
Worcester; Thomas Langly, Bishop of Durham—
all Cardinals. Were they really Bishops of these
English sees, or weren't they really Cardinals?
What a Cardinal has to do with Rome, and Rome's
Pope, all the world knows: they are above all others
Pope's men; his Privy Councillors, his electoral
princes, his hands and arms and eyes and ears. He
was one of them, one of them will take his place,
when his death voids it. Next to the Pope himself
nothing more papal conceivable than a Cardinal—
a very stale truism, certainly, what a cardinal has to
do with the Pope—but a very unanswerable question
what he has to do with Anglican continuity.

This Henry Beaufort, of the title of Sant Eusebio,
Cardinal of the Holy Roman Church, has there
ever been question that he was in fact and truth
Bishop of Winchester? Here his effigy lies upon
his tomb; yonder in the fields still stands his benefac-
tion of St. Cross; 'tis as holder of this see he lies
here. No one ever doubted he was Bishop here,
and no one doubts he was one of the Pope's
Cardinals. To what Church belonged this Card-

inal? Or did he belong to one Church, and his
flock and clergy to another. Was he "Roman,"
and were they "Anglican"? Common-sense and
plain, indifferent history know he was Cardinal, and
prince of the Roman Church: does history pretend
he was no true Bishop here, or that the diocese he
ruled here, its clergy, and its people, held another
faith from his, and held him for an alien and schismatic, they belonging to one Church and he to
another and a foreign one? Or can any man doubt
to what Church the Cardinal of Sant Eusebio belonged, to what faith he professed obedience before
he received yonder red hat? That he preceded Dr.
Wilberforce as occupant of this episcopal throne no
one pretends to doubt: can anyone pretend to believe
that he was Dr. Wilberforce's predecessor in a
common faith; that the Church of that waggish
divine was also *his* Church: that what the nineteenth
century prelate believed *he* believed, and (what may
be as much to the point) that what the nineteenth
century prelate disbelieved he disbelieved too?

If anyone can believe all that, one readily under-
stands what is meant by saying that faith is the
faculty of believing what one knows to be impossible.

Or was Winchester a Papal island in an Anglican
sea: all England else duly Anglican, this one diocese
"Roman"? In sooth there must have been a
"Roman" archipelago in this England, or Canter-
bury never had those nine Cardinal-Primates, nor
York those three, and Luxemburgh was never
Bishop of Ely, Repingdon of Lincoln, Pandulph

of Norwich, Hallum of Salisbury, Thoresby of Worcester, Langley of Durham, or the Blessed Fisher of Rochester.

And the Pope Adrian? Was he no true member of the Catholic Church in England of his day, or had he abjured the island-church of his baptism before grasping Peter's heavy keys? Was he Anglican or "Roman"? A twelfth century Pope is commonly accounted pretty Roman, and, as history has been written so far, Adrian has never been presented to the world as an Anglican Antipope.

Till the devout holders of "Continuity" have proved that Pope Adrian was an Anglican on Peter's throne, or a renegade to Papal faith and the Papal Church; till they have demonstrated that Henry Beaufort was no Cardinal, or that he was never Bishop of Winchester; if they had nothing else to prove, they must support patiently the smile of common-sense at their wistful, forlorn hope of a claim. If Wilberforce's effigy, between its six supporting angels, could smile, I warrant it would, and pretty broadly, at anyone who should assure him that he and his predecessor, the Cardinal, belonged to the same Church and held the same creed. He was a man of insupportable common-sense, with an intolerable capacity for recognising the very bores of theory—beastly facts.

POLE, CRANMER, AND CONTINUITY

THE admirers of Continuity are far from denying that the Church, as it was in England under the Plantagenets, was Catholic, that it was Catholic under the Lancastrian and Yorkist kings, under Henry VII., and at the accession of Henry VIII.: during all of which time it was in communion with the Pope, and with all the other Churches under his obedience, with the Papal Churches of France, Spain, Italy, Sicily, Sardinia, Corsica, Poland, Austria, etc., and professed in matters of Faith precisely what they all professed. No one, Continuity-folk or otherwise, denies, or is concerned to deny, that so far all these people, of different race, language, and country, were Catholics, belonging to one Church under one visible head.

Then there arrived the English Reformation, the result of which was that the English Church discarded the Pope and his communion, and also discarded a great mass of belief integral to the Church, of which he was the visible head. If it be correct to say that the Pope was a Roman Catholic it is also correct to say that all the Cardinals, Archbishops, Bishops, prelates, abbots, priests, monks, nuns, and lay people who were in communion with him in France, Spain, Italy, and so on, were Roman Catholics too: he did not belong to one Church and religion and they to another. And it must equally be said that the Archbishops, bishops, etc., who occupied the English Sees when Henry VIII. mounted the throne were Roman Catholics; they had one Faith with the Pope, and belonged to the Church which everywhere acknowledged him as its visible head. When the time arrived in which the English Church fell out of Communion with the Pope, and with all those under his obedience over the seas, and ceased to teach what he and they taught, then, according to their own belief, and that of all the world besides, its members were no longer members of his Church, and their religion was no longer the same as his. They had a Church of their own, of which the Pope was not the head, and a religion of their own which had discarded a mass of that teaching integral to all the Churches in communion with Rome. They were no longer Roman Catholics: they no longer belonged to the same Church and the same religion to which foreign Roman Catholics belonged. They had changed their religion. According to the Continuity-folk they were, however, Catholics, though not Roman Catholics. What had they been in their youth? Only Roman Catholics? And was the profession of Protestantism necessary to Catholicise them? If, we must say again, the "reformed" Church of England was Catholic, then the Catholic Church existed only in England, and had ceased everywhere else: for indubitably the reformed religion of England was not the religion of any other country in the world. The Churches of Catholic Europe had, elsewhere, ceased to be Catholic: they had done nothing, but had changed, and lost their Catholicity. They had discarded nothing, innovated nothing, but had changed; while the English Church, that had innovated and discarded right and left, was left serenely unchanged, Catholic still! But even in England there were those who changed nothing, and innovated nothing: did Sir Thomas More die a Catholic? did Cardinal Fisher? or had they fallen into mere Roman Catholicism? At what date did they change their religion from Catholic to Roman Catholic? Cardinal Pole and Cranmer were both Archbishops of Canterbury: which was the Catholic? No human being has ever believed they both belonged to the same religion at the time of their respective deaths; everybody knows they had belonged to the same religion as children; which changed? Was Cranmer burnt because he was a Catholic? Was it Catholicity of which he signed the retractation with that right hand, which, according to Macaulay's ruthless gibe, must shine with peculiar brilliancy in heaven? I know that Cranmer will never be canonised if he has to wait for a Continuity Pope to do it: the Continuity-folk do not like him. Is it because he was a Protestant?—a Protestant Primate of a Church that has always been, and is still, Catholic?—whose other Primates were all Catholic—like Whitgraft, Tillotson, Secker, and the rest!

Anyway, Cranmer and Pole, though both brought up in the same Church, did not belong to the same Church during the reign of Edward VI. If Cranmer was the Catholic during Edward's reign, Pole wasn't. When did he leave the Catholic Church? *He* had changed nothing from his birth, how was his religion changed over his head? Catholicity must be an odd concern if it sticks to us when we alter our faith and slips from us when we don't. If the Continuity-folk have the right idea of Catholicity, then was Catholicity unknown till the Protestant Reformation introduced it into England, had never been known in any other land or age, and has, with some insular prejudice, confined itself to England and her dependencies ever since—*a l'insu* to all the rest of the world, Christian or heathen, Jewish, Islamic, Hindu, Buddhist, Atheist, or Agnostic, that has always laboured under the delusion that the Pope was a Catholic, and that those of his obedience belonged to his Church, while those who belonged to religious bodies refusing his obedience were not members of his Church, and were not Catholics.

Had the English Reformers themselves recked of "Continuity," they might well have devoted an Article of the Church of England's faith to it: and made up the forty—a more mystic number, with less anti-apostolic associations, for the thirty-nine are suggestive chiefly of the forty stripes save one five times suffered by St. Paul at the hands of those to whom Christian faith was odious. "A fond thing vainly invented" they might have called it, like five of the Church's sacraments. And then the Protestant Catholics would have been *sure* it was all right, for nothing endears a proposition so much to your Protestant Catholic as that it should stand utterly condemned by the most authoritative definitions of faith promulgated by the founders of his religion.

THE CONTINUITY TRIBUTE

WHAT, then, does the Continuity plea really mean? That is a question which it is worth while asking ourselves before we leave this subject. The plea itself is one which no one will admit except those by whom it is made: it is made not by a Church, or by a religion, but by a mere section of a Church, by a small minority of the members of a numerous religious body. That large portion of the Established Church which is still perfectly content with the name of Protestant is not at all anxious to claim identity with the unreformed religion as it existed in England at the accession of Henry VIII., and this is true not only of the extreme Low Church party in the Church of England, but equally true of the much larger moderate section, which is, probably, as little attracted by violent Low Churchism as it is by Ritualism. The Anglican who likes "nice" services in church, who prefers to have pretty flowers on the altar and sees no harm in a cross as a centrepiece, or indeed in a pair of candlesticks flanking the cross, or in a coloured stole; who is accustomed to see those in the chancel turn eastward during the Creed, and all the *Gloria Patri,* and does not care whether a clergyman's head is covered

at a rainy funeral by a biretta or a college-cap—
that sort of Anglican not only dislikes the somewhat
obsolete ugliness and bareness of old-time Protestanism, but he is also slightly scornful of ritualistic
"mummeries and millinery," of Roman importa-
tions, in the way of dress and ceremonial, and he is
entirely unconvinced by "Roman teaching" pro-
pounded to him as the real faith of the Church to
which he and his have belonged for several centuries.
He is certain that such teaching in pulpits occupied
by clergymen of the Church of England is new and
alien.   The extreme Low Churchman, the more
moderate Evangelical, the "ordinary Churchman,"
and the Broad Churchman are all agreed in one
conviction—that the Church of England did at the
Reformation renounce the Catholic doctrines in
force when the Reformation came: that the old
religion of England, under the Plantagenets, for
instance, was Roman Catholic, and that the
Reformation gave England a new religion which
was not Catholic but Protestant.

And this was recognised, outside England, and has
been recognised ever since, by all those who, as
outsiders, were unconcerned, and had nothing to do
in the matter, but merely saw and acknowledged
an obvious fact: the plain fact that England had
turned Protestant, and had abjured Catholicity as
a nation.   That fact was no more apparent to the
foreign Catholics, who had made no change, than it
was to the foreign Protestants who had made new
religions of their own, and to those who never had

belonged to the Catholic Church, Jews, Mahome-
tans, and so on.

All this we have said, and all this is perfectly
well known to the world at large.

What then does the Plea of Continuity mean?

That a plea so quaint, so blind to every consideration of mere fact, should be advanced at all, must
point to something.   What does it mean?

To us it seems that the answer to that question
is both simple and touching.   The plea is a tribute,
none the less significant because it is involuntary and
reluctant.

For a long time it pleased those who had with-
drawn themselves from Catholic unity and Catholic obedience to vilify and deride the name of
Catholic.   They justified their own change by a
rancorous abuse of that which they had abandoned.
They spared no condemnation of the Catholic teaching and of the Church that taught it.   Nothing
would have been felt by them as a fouler insult
than such an assertion (if anyone had ventured on
an assertion so preposterous) as that they had
changed nothing, but were still bound by the old rule
of faith; that the Reformation meant no more for
England than the Council of Trent meant for the
Catholics of the Continent.   To be Catholic they
held to be damnable, to be Protestant was their
national glory: Englishman and Protestant meant
the same thing: to be Catholic was to be foreign,
un-English, a taint of disloyalty, a bend sinister on
the escutcheon of patriotism.

And the Plea of Continuity is Time's reprisal. The vilified name of Catholic is envied, and, as far as may be, stolen. After all the black abuse of Catholicity, a campaign of calumny over three hundred years old, there is something, after all, so great and incommunicable in the name of Catholic that descendants of those who would fain have obliterated it are wistfully clutching at it, in spite of all evidence of fact and common sense, as if the mere name were something to conjure Heaven with!

God is one, and His truth is one: that was the great promulgation of Catholicity: it was the family secret of the Hebrew Church. To the outside Heathen world, with many gods, it was a new idea, and by it Christianity conquered paganism. Multiform heathenism would never have succumbed to a multiform Christian Church. The uncaring, indifferent pagan might gibe at the Catholic intolerance of heresy, but it was the unity of Catholic faith that alone would destroy the vague, all-tolerating, subdivided polytheism, and did destroy it. As soon as Christianity divided against itself, paganism and polytheism began the revival of which we are witnessing the fruits. Paganism will never lie conquered under the vague and multiform theories of a Christianity that tolerates divided teaching within itself. Christianity that is not Catholic is only sectarian and Paganism will not admit superiority in any sect of any name: its only superior and conqueror has been Catholicity that holds to the hard fact—One only God and one only truth about Him.

Paganism is the new preoccupation of the new world, as it preoccupied the world when Catholicism came and ousted it.

Those who put forth this faltering plea of Continuity are aware of it. They know well that the Reformation undid the work of fifteen centuries; they are bitterly ashamed of it; and the only thing they can see to do is to ignore it, as far as their own country and Church is concerned, and, in spite of notorious and dismal fact, deny it.

The Church Catholic did what no Protestant Churches have done, or could do. And the Continuity people are so deeply sensitive of it that they can only cry out "We are Catholics. The Church of the One God *must* be Catholic. So we belong to it. We always did: we and those who split off from it (they never *could* have done anything so ruinous and frightful; filial piety forbids our confessing they did so horrible a thing). You do not understand us, nor our Church: you will not realise that in calling themselves Protestant our forefathers meant 'Catholic' all the time. As for us, we utterly abjure the ugly, disastrous name of Protestant. We like all you like, we loathe the heresies you loathe: look at our altars, our vestments, our incense, our very rosaries and Benedictions of the Blessed Sacrament! Is all that Protestant? Are we not eagerly bringing back all those things our fathers—no they didn't banish them: they—"

Can they look around them, and look back, back such a little way, and say that all these things have always been a part of the religion established in England at the Reformation?

Can a country have a Protestant *religion* and a Catholic *Church*? Were the bishops, who ousted the old Catholic bishops, Catholic in religion? Were their successors Protestant in faith or Catholic?

What would have happened to a pre-Reformation bishop in England (or anywhere else) who taught what the bishops of the English Church have been teaching these three hundred years and more? Has any bishop, any dean, any clergyman, ever been turned out of the English Church for teaching Protestanism? And in the Catholic Church abroad, admitted to be Catholic by the Continuity people *there,* could any bishop, or prelate, or priest, teach Protestantism and be suffered to remain where he was?

Has any portion of the Catholic Church of the Continent taught Protestant heresy during a century and remained a part, a branch of the Catholic Church? That the English Church taught Protestant heresy throughout the eighteenth century no one as yet denied: to the Continuity plea it is necessary to say that a national religion and a national Church are different things: that those who belong to the national religion may be all Protestant, and the Church to which they belong be altogether Catholic.

APOSTOLIC WITNESS

WHAT Catholics mean when they say that the true Church of Christ must be not only One, Holy and Universal, but also Apostolic, they know very well. A Catholic child knows: but it is by no means certain that non-Catholics in general know. What is more probable is that our idea of an Apostolic Church is not attractive to them.

To certain High Anglicans it is so far attractive that they are aggrieved if we do not admit their claim to Apostolicity by which *they* mean, apparently, no more than that the clergy of the Established Church have, as they maintain, an unbroken spiritual descent through ordination by duly consecrated bishops from the Apostles. But the High Anglicans are only a section even of their own Church; and a great number even of the clergy of the Church of England are very little interested in this claim, because its tenability or non-tenability is immaterial to their position. Still less do the rank and file of the laity of their Church concern themselves with the matter.

Outside the Establishment the Protestant feeling is, on the whole, worse than indifferent to Apostolicity, even in the United Anglican sense. To immense numbers of those who belong to the Free Christian Churches the idea of a clergy claiming apostolic descent is simply repellent, as involving that sacerdotalism which they hold in abhorrence. Some, at least, of these Free Churches have no clergy at all; no doubt "Christian Scientists," for instance, consider themselves Christians; but they certainly do not want any priests with Apostolic Descent. And there are innumerable sects who want them just as little: not only among the newest, but also among the older religious bodies.

Probably the vast majority of Protestants, far from envying the Apostolicity claimed by the Catholic Church, regard it with repugnance, and consider it one of the Church's blemishes and drawbacks.

And the reason that underlies this attitude towards Apostolicity is precisely that which is at the root of their dislike of Unity, Sanctity, and Catholicity, as notes of a Church.   For Apostolicity, quite as truly as the other three notes, is not reconcilable with Private Judgement.

How could Mrs. Eddy found a religion, how could *anybody*, at this time of day, if Apostolicity were an essential?   And the foundation of new religions is a very seductive occupation: a field of activity that the modern world loves to keep open to all comers. To originate a sect is one of the easiest ways of achieving a certain measure of importance.   To become even a political leader is more difficult, and, perhaps more expensive, though the expense is less than it used to be. To be a demagogue calls for hardly any capital; nor does it necessitate very high intellectual endowments: but it demands adroitness, sleight of speech, a thick skin, an indifference to results that might stagger men of even a very commonplace conscientiousness and a power of seducing the ear and fancy of large bodies of men. You can found a sect even though you be able to get round only a handful of old women. Your intellectual capital may be sheer beggary: you may have merely a parlour voice, that would not carry twenty yards out of doors; you need not be funny, even vulgarly funny, though it will help you if you are; you may lack even that knowledge of men that consists in a deft instinctive perception of human greed and appetite, that consists indeed in taking for granted that the ears of a crowd will be apt receivers of the message of your own spite, envy, and maliciousness.

It would be hard to conceive of any single attribute of ordinary leadership of which it could be said that without it no one could found a sect. The most blatant demagogue must not *seem* silly; but no one's silliness need keep him back from originating a sect. A demagogue must have a *large* following; but the smaller sect is often the pleasantest to handle, and is apt to be rather pleased by the notion that it is a "little flock." The prudent sectary has no idea of a universal appeal. He (or she) knows better than to aim at anything which could answer to the needs of all men of every race and tongue. He only aspires to be the hero of a group: and it may be local, and must be idiosyn-cratic. But Apostolicity would ruin him: and he knows it.

Of course, some religious innovators have been rich in the gifts of demagogy, Luther was, Knox was, Calvin was: Cranmer was not, but Latimer was.

And some sect-founders, having some of the demagogue's adroitness, have aimed at, and secured, large audiences and strong "following." Others, with slightly different gifts, have also known how to tickle many ears. They may have possessed but a shallow intellectual equipment; what they did possess was a shewd, instinctive perception of some phase in the character of their own time. Mrs. Eddy, for instance; she was clearly not a woman of high mental capacity; she was without culture, and her spiritual sense was obtuse. Even religiosity was with her no life-long hobby, which established habit had taught her to ride with practised judgment. But she was shrewd, and she was perceptive enough to be aware that her age was morbidly neurotic. The assimilation of that meagre discovery was sufficient for her purpose, and she exploited it with results that might amaze even Carlyle's pessimistic estimate of human wisdom.

Christian Science could not have been founded in the Middle Ages; because, with many faults (all duly insisted upon now) they were not in the least neurotic. But Mrs. Eddy, if the choice had been left to her, would have been far too sharp to have been born in the Middle Ages. Fate favoured her; and she adorned the age of patent-medicines, the drug-habit, morphomaniacs, Nursing Homes, and health-faddists.

Here was a field *asking* for a general specialist and she stepped forward with a prescription of engaging simplicity. Her success was, and is, phenomenal; but how if Apostolicity had mattered sixpence to her patients?

There are worse sects than hers; but the same incubus would have smothered them also. Shakers, Spiritualists, Swedenborgians, Latterday Saints— and so on for as long as you like—what on earth would have happened to them if this little tedious note of Apostolicity had been held, like a pistol, at what the poverty of the English language allows us to call the heads of their originators?

Then again—that very word brings us up against the root of the objection. A modern sect must seem to embody some sort of "originality," something of a new discovery; and there is nothing "original" in Apostolicity. The "doctrine and tradition of the Apostles" squashes originality in religion: and sectarian faddism won't be squashed.

Mr. Pecksniff's feelings would not consent to be smothered like the young princes in the Tower: the more he pressed the bolster on them, the more they looked round the corner of it. So with the modern faddists of religiosity: the Apostolic note would be their bolster: the Doctrine and Tradition of the Apostles would smother them—if they would endure its application: but they won't, and the more you tried to press it on them, the more would they gurgle and choke, and goggle wistfully round the corner of it. For the ·Apostolic note stands for precisely what they do not want: its function is that of perpetual and incorruptible witness of God's declared will in belief and practice, and what they like is to express a new and half-formed opinion of their own.

Non desideriis hominum, sed voluntate Dei wrote Cardinal York on his medals of his own royalty. The doctrine and tradition of the Apostles stands as indefectible reminder of the will of God in the sphere of faith and morals: and what the novelty monger in religion wants is no such reminder, but a free hand in the promulgation of the desires of men. The unity of the Church is the necessary result, and the reflex of the Unity of God, and is therefore intolerable to peoples who have clearly abandoned the idea of one objectively existent God, and have really adopted the idea of many very different subjectively existent Gods, American Gods, gods adapted to Anglo-Saxon, German, or Swedish tastes in religion; gods for the wise, supercultured gods, and vulgar gods.

And the Apostolic note insists on the changelessness of God; whereas the modern sectarian fancy reflects its own unstable love of change in the ever-changing god whose feeble portrait it is forever painting and blurring, smudging and repainting, in the thinly disguised effort at self-deification.

IN EXCUSE OF SILENCE

IT was, apparently, a consolation to many people suffering from the shock of Cardinal Newman's submission to Rome to say that he wished himself back again.   As a child I was constantly assured by very honest persons that this was notoriously the case; and I cannot believe that they would have said it unless they really thought it.   Being a peculiar child, for a Protestant, it caused in me a feeling of antagonism to the great Oratorian; he had possessed himself of a treasure I envied, and, if this were true, he wanted to be rid of it.   How far I was convinced that the report really *was* true I cannot pretend to say for certain now—much more than forty years afterwards; but I doubt if I was fully convinced, for even a child knows that people will assume, without much question, that to be a fact which they desire should be a fact, and I could perceive that it was felt to be a heavy slur on the Church of England that Newman should have found himself constrained to leave it.   To believe that he had repented at leisure, that he was disappointed in the Catholic Church and disillusioned, and would fain return whence he came, was a strong comfort to those who had that belief.

That the thing should ever have been said at all

may not be surprising; for Newman's name was one around which report was apt to fly: it was the stormy petrel of rumour, conjecture, and assertion. And the un-Catholic world never has been able to realise how much discussion is freely indulged among Catholics, how much individual character and taste are allowed their natural and legitimate play; it seems to be assumed, outside, that all really loyal Catholics are cast in one mould, made to one pattern, and, because they hold the same faith, have also precisely the same way of looking at everything—at politics, at devotional methods, at matters of taste, at each and all of the thousand questions that every day and week, month and year, bring into consideration.

Because, for instance, Newman was known to hold very strong views about university education, and that they were not the views of Archbishop Manning, it was promptly assumed that he was not in sympathy with Catholic opinion; and because it was also known that he *had* sympathisers, it was immediately asserted that he held a sort of sectarian position. With great glee it was concluded that the position was one of wistful leanings of an Anglican tinge—that he longed to be home again in the bosom of the Church for which his enormous influence had done so much.

It was a human feeling enough, and honest enough, maybe, in the beginning; but how any honest person who believed a word that Newman could say or write, who held *him* to be honest, could go on

making the same assertion after Newman's letter to
the Duke of Norfolk, it is very difficult to understand. That he should have felt himself constrained
to make that disclaimer of regret for his change
from Anglicanism to Catholicity, must have seemed
to him cruel. That there should be any, the least,
necessity to put on record his never-wavering
gratitude to God for the grace that had brought him
into the Church must have seemed to him out-
rageous. But no disclaimer could have been more
simple, solemn, frank, and convincing; no record
could be more monumental in its plain brevity, direct-
ness, and sufficiency. It should have sufficed even
those who had never been at the pains to read his
Apologia, or any, indeed, of the works he wrote as
a Catholic. Nevertheless, the old assertion was
still made; was made, no doubt, after he had become
a Cardinal; may, for aught I know, be made now.
Similar assertions will, perhaps, go on being made
concerning any convert to "Rome" whose passing
thither is felt to be a sword-thrust between the ribs
of Protestantism.

It is a weak effort at revenge for a fact that must
always be disconcerting: the fact that converts to
Rome are commonly those who have been striving
to have the highest ideal of the Church of England;
who have been most eager to believe her Catholic;
the most earnest in their endeavour to live a supernatural life by grace of her sacraments. That a
man who cares at all for the ideal of a Church
should come to confess that it is not to be found in

that of England; that he who thinks it an essential of true and full Christianity to be Catholic should be forced to the conviction that Anglicanism is not Catholicity, but only a more ornate Protestantism; that one who has grasped the fact that, by Christ's institution, sacramental life is necessary to supernatural life on earth, should feel himself constrained to declare that the Church which has always possessed all seven sacraments is their true and natural home, and that five are really missing in the Church of England—all this must be really offensive to such as are still willing to content themselves with Anglicanism and their own somewhat eccentric position in it. To such it must come as a pleasant reprisal to assert, and believe if they can, that he who has left them for "Rome" has not found in Rome what he went to seek; that there he has experienced, not the realization of his ideal, but its shattering and failure.

And there is, besides, the great, not particularly Anglican, bulk of stolid Protestantism, heavily moribund, but not deprived of the faculty of speech, which clings still to outworn, obsolete, dull misrepresentations, and likes to go on declaring that Catholicity is really bad, immoral, and wicked. In *their* care the only scandal is that a good man (no one gabbles more of goodness than they who think it slightly impious to call anyone good) should turn to Rome as to a fit and safe instructress in piety and morals. So to them also it is a satisfaction to believe that the deluded creature who aimed at goodness and sought help in "Rome" should find himself cozened, and secretly long for escape from its sink of iniquities. To neither party does it seem to occur that he who could change once might with even greater facility change again; that he who was able to cut himself loose from lifelong associations, affections, tastes, predilections, for conscience' sake, might very easily fling off new and strange fetters, abhorred and not beloved, strange, irksome, and resented, and be free again. I was always assured as a child and young boy that Newman would be a Protestant again if he could, but no one mentioned why he could not. "Ah! he longs to come back—if they would let him," was the formula.

It was odd that I never pictured him immured in the dungeons of the Holy Office, but I never did. Perhaps some did. It is one of the finest joys of innocent Protestantism to imagine every medieval power of the Papacy in full and unrestrained operation, in spite of that practical abolition of the Papacy in which they also complacently believe.

Converts to Catholicity are often twitted with their fondness for writing books about their conversion: it seems to me that the sort of habit we have been noticing provides of itself a sufficient excuse, if any excuse be necessary. It proves the naturalness and legitimacy of their attitude, who, having made such a change, wish to give a reasonable account of it, and desire, incidentally, to show their satisfaction in the change, and on what that comfort and satisfaction is grounded. Nevertheless, to write such books must, as I think, be very difficult, must even be very painful, and only to be done at a sharp personal cost. To be done at all it must involve a self-revelation, an opening of hidden and sacred recesses of the heart and spirit, from which we shrink with a sort of horror and repugnance that is almost decency. No doubt there is a temperament to which it is easier to make the in-visible, impersonal public a confidant than it would be to confide in almost any individual; poets can sing aloud to all the world things they could never bring themselves to say to a brother or a friend in the most secure privacy. But not everyone has that tempera-ment; to most of us the public is of all audiences the most horrible. And of all the things we may have to confide, those are the least easy to speak of which concern the inner motions of our own spirit, our ways of thinking about God, His ways of dealing with us, spiritual episodes, our own religious growth and stagnation, our starts and standings still, our hurries and delays in all that inward life of ours which is a natural secret.

Supposing a man able to write at all, and suppos-ing him to feel under some obligation, or impulse, to write thus of his own intimate matters, it would seem to me that he would usually try to veil himself under some shape of fiction. To his natural reticence it would appear less repugnant to say what he desired, not as of himself, but as of some imaginary personage. Thus do poets, who, for the most part, confess themselves through the mouths of many third persons.   And thus, I think, most would choose to act who had a spiritual tale to tell, a soul's story to embody.   It relieves them of the incubus-sense of egoism, and it leaves them immensely more free.   For a man setting about such a narration of himself *in propria persona* must be appalled by the fear of seeming to make himself out a more spiritual person than he knows himself to be—perhaps a sort of saint, since the stupid are apt to confound spiritual experiences with sanctity, and he is aware that stupid readers are seldom in a complete minority.   The picture he has to present *must* be partly one-sided; it shows in general only the spiritual and higher side; while decency forbids him to parade the other side—the lower, the side of his sins and shortcomings; he is half afraid of seeming, even to himself, a hypocrite.

By telling his story as of some other fictitious personage, he is saved all this scruple and bondage.   He can write with more reality and fuller truth, though the form of his narration is fictional, and a more genuine revelation is possible. Neither Rousseau nor Montaigne were morbidly reticent; the former was morbidly unreticent; the latter, if he lacked morbidity, had also a lack of the faculty of decency: I suspect that both would have left the world a revelation of themselves as vivid and sincere, more just and more complete, if the *Confessions* and the autobiography wrapped up in the *Essays* had been embodied in the form of fiction.   It is certainly not intended to put in comparison the two books just cited with those accounts of their conversion which converts have given us *in propria persona*.   The motive of the two former is utterly opposed to the motive of the latter.   The *Confessions* of Rousseau and the *Essays* of Montaigne are monuments of egoism that can be compared   only to the pyramids; the latter are only accused of egoism by superficial and unsympathetic criticism; they are intended as gifts to a cause, are offered in payment of a debt; the speaker is not the hero of the piece, but its chorus: the real hero is the Catholic Church, and it is *her* justification that is really meant, not the speaker's own. Each of these several works, though made by many men, aim at one thing—to illustrate the various and legitimate attraction of Catholic truth for minds of every cast.   If anyone can do it, it is a good and useful work, obnoxious to no sincere objection of vanity or self-absorption.   For myself, I doubt if I could do it.   Many times I have been asked to do it, sometimes by direct and private application, sometimes by public suggestion—as recently in a review of a book of mine called Gracechurch:

We are tantalised (says the reviewer) by his (the author's) references to his religious life as a child, and we wish he could have seen his way to expand them.   The making of a Churchman—beginning, as in this instance, in a boy's search for the religious help he felt himself to need— is a subject of psychological interest, and deserves a better place than the odd pages modestly assigned to it in these sketches.

That is a frank and cordial invitation. It deserves, perhaps, a response as frank and cordial. Catholic and very friendly readers have urged the same thing, as a duty, on the author of the book. But I think them all mistaken. A man can only do what God has given him the power of doing. The power to strip himself of the shield and veil of fiction, and still be frank, sincere, unaffected; to stand, naked and unashamed, unclad in that innocent mask and disguise of fiction, has been, this writer thinks, withheld from him. An author may often be deceived as to what he can do; it is seldom he is wrong in his convictions as to what is quite beyond him. Did St. Philip say: "Brothers, let us make fools of ourselves for Jesus Christ?" Anyway he never made himself anything in the least like a fool. It may be a duty to do what is impossible—but only when One Voice gives the command, as when the man whose arm was withered was told by pitying Omnipotence to stretch it out. To go beyond one's impotence may be to go beyond one's grace, and we need not attempt it because a kindly critic, or eager friends, urge it as a literary or a religious duty.

Another friendly, and unknown, voice from over the great and bitter water that divides this Old World, to which I belong, from that New World, whither I can adventure only in a hundred disguises of fiction, came to me of late begging that I would write, for a book to be made up of such revelations, my reasons for being glad of being what I am—like a very different some one—"after all a child of the

Church." So many thousands of words were conceded to me for the telling—but, ah! how few they
seemed! I suppose the world itself, with all its
myriad tongues, contains not words enough for such
a telling as that. How attempt it? How dare I—
for sheer reverence? Perhaps five-and-thirty years
ago I could have set down for any man to read the
causes of my gladness and gratefulness for being a
Catholic; it was a new country then, and first impres-
sions are sharp and easily noted: the traveller in a
strange land is alert to perceive and tell things, and
true things, that escape the attention of men who
have always dwelt there. To another traveller,
following him, it seems that he knew the land well
—because both of them knew it so little.

On that October morning, five-and-thirty years
ago, when I could hardly believe (like Thomas *prae
gaudio*) that I was a Catholic, and asked some one
if I really were and was answered, "As truly a Catholic as the Pope," then, perhaps, I thought I knew
what it was to be one and could have told out, or
written down for anyone who demanded it, what
cause I had for all my exultant joy; why it was that
the sun shone differently on a new and gladsome
world, and every autumn leaf seemed a syllable in a
chorus of whispering congratulation, and every little
breath of crisp October air was saying, gleefully, in
my ear, "You are a Catholic—a Catholic."

No doubt I thought I knew why: with the alphabet of my gladness in my hands I never suspected
all the million words those few baby letters would

come to spell. But *after* five-and-thirty years! Eh! how little was it that I knew of the meanings of being a Catholic at the beginning of them—how impossible to tell it all at the end of them, when one knows so much more. To snatch an instance: I thought, then, that I knew how to hear Mass, and it was years before I knew. Dare I, for reverence, try to write down in cold print what hearing Mass is? No doubt he said truly, in one sense, who told me, "You are a Catholic as truly as the Pope." But there is another sense, in which one may say as truly that no one can become a Catholic in a minute, nor in a year; that it takes many years, slow and reverent, patient and listening, whereof every day and week is a lesson, or a group of lessons, wherein one is always learning, learning—ah! and unlearning— many a mistake and hurried misapprehension, so shall we die neophytes at last: but simpler, humbler, than we began.

How slowly, with what reverence, has the Church unfolded, leaf by leaf, all the trees of her Divine teaching that Christ laid in her breast an indestructible seed; and how few lives are long enough, patient enough, to assimilate, as bone of their bone and flesh of their flesh, that food of knowledge. All the great heresiarchs choked themselves with hurry and haste: too irreverent to wait till the half-truth they had snatched at should be exorcised of its half-falsehood, with blatant stumbling arrogance they proclaimed it the very truth itself, and became liars teaching a lie.

And is this not why those who have been Catholics many years seldom write of what they gained by conversion? It is not, maybe, the reason assumed by critics hostile to the Church. To them it is easier to say that they who are old converts are no longer enamoured of the mistress whose faults they have learned; that to the old convert Catholicity has grown stale, and the beauties of Catholicity have dwindled down to paint and tinsel, not very moving at near hand; that the old convert keeps his mouth shut because he would not be let open it, for fear he should tell too plain a truth.

But such a shallow, dull accusation of critics whom nothing will make candid or friendly, will not vex us. The young lover may be a glib sonneteer of his mistress's eyebrow; but he to whom she has been wedded half a lifetime writes no sonnets—though his love is deeper, stronger, faithfuller, more reverent, because he knows what once he only hoped. No fourteen lines could knit up all he might say; and, for reverence of her, he will hold his peace, lest his stammering eulogies should do her an injustice.

Our Lady the Church, whose face was all we knew once, is beyond our praise; and we shrink from betraying our own inadequacy, and hold our peace; though still it is well that the young sonneteer should sing and fill the world with echoes that keep it sweeter; his praise of beauty reminds of truth, for his song means always this, that "God is one and His Church is one; and she is His mirror, wherein, by every shifting light is caught, and caught again, some reflection of His Supreme Beauty."

PAX

I REMEMBER with what vehement, though necessarily silent, protest I first heard, in church, that Easter is the greatest of all Festivals: when one is seven or eight years old the Resurrection Feast cannot appeal like that of Christ's human birth. Death has never drawn near; the life we know here looks illimitable, and those whom we love seem immortal like ourselves: some of them are, perhaps, already old, most of them are much older than ourselves, but they appear to us to be fixed in their respective ages: they are big boys and girls, young men and women, middle-aged folk, and old people, and we only remember them as they are: in our memory they have hardly changed, and we cannot imagine them changing, least of all do we realise the change that will take some of them away from our sight altogether.

But we have a memory already, and it enshrines chiefly things outside our own short-shadowed experience: the Bible stories are as real to us in childhood as those that elder persons treasure, half wistfully, all tenderly, out of their own lengthening past. And of all those exquisite tales the loveliest is that of Bethlehem. Perhaps it is the first a child learns, and it should be. Once heard, it brings God down

to us, and lifts us to Him: there can be no aloofness
between a little child and the Christ of whom he first
thinks as of a Divine baby in an adoring mother's
arms.   I do not believe a grown man ever betters
upon the picture of Bethlehem he first drew in his
mind from his own mother's tender, simple description.   It is one that simplicity and tenderness can
best describe; no eloquence or fine phrasing can
make it more real, more human, or more Divine.
The scene is homely and humble, and the figures of
its groups, poor folk all of them, of no unfamiliar
grandeur or worldly consequence.   The poverty of
the stable has no bleakness, the starlit night no chill,
for the listening child.   To him that midnight can
never seem dark, but shining out of a past that
seems but yesterday, sacred, not aloof, with the
light that never was on sea or land.   And learning
that ineffable story the child needs not to be told
that God is Love; he knows it for always.   And the
Christmas gladness is more than earthly; he feels
all the world to be the Christ-Child's church, the
wintry fields by Bethlehem its sanctuary and chancel,
the singing angels its carol-choir, the crib its altar.
All the joyous greetings have a ring like that of the
bells that fling the Christmas message through the
clear and frozen air; the Christmas gifts are more
than mere presents—they are sacred and mysterious;
the child can never think they were bought with
common money in any common shop; the other Child
sent them from Bethlehem, and they are holy from
His fingers.   Christmas games are not like games of

other seasons; they are wonderful and full of a strange joyousness, as though among the rest, unseen but intimately felt, the Child from Heaven were playing too. The very laughter of Christmas is only an echo of the silver-throated bells, and the bells themselves are but echoing on the Angel's hymn of glory and peace.

So was Christmas to us long ago, in the far-away years before the hard noon of life came upon us, before the world meant anything worse to us than the lovely word God's creating whisper spelled, when sin meant to us only a naughtiness that was itself innocent, and the devil was a terror to us, unimaginable as a friend. So is it now to millions of children who have to-day all the wisdom we have unlearned in the crowded school of folly. To children Merry Christmas! Mirth and Christmas are theirs by special right of fitness, and happiest is our own Christmas when we can help to make theirs all that we remember ours to have been once. A season of peculiar unselfishness, our best hope of finding it still happy ourselves must lie in the endeavour to make it so to others. To try in later life doggedly to reconstruct what is unalterably past can yield us only disappointment and disillusion; he who says within himself, *This Christmas shall be as the old ones: good cheer and jocund doings shall bring back the joys we remember,* must fail. A world-aged man's Christmas cannot be as the child's. Many strive to forget this, and their failure makes them bitter, ready to carp and grumble at the holy sweet season, as sweet and holy still as when they themselves were holy and sweet.

Our Christmas, who have half a hundred behind us, must be full of memories, not impersonal as a child's, but strung together out of our own gathered rosary of experience, joyful, mysterious, and sorrowful, not many glorious. And the joyful ones themselves take a tinge of wistfulness as they shine out of an ever-lengthening past. We sit alone, and unforgotten figures arise to greet us, smilingly, but with smiles that have grown unearthly, for their light is not hence, but the reflection of what falls upon their faces in a holy place where we are not with them.

"The least gift that they left to our childhood in long ago
    years
Is changed from a toy to a relic, and gazed at through
    crystals of tears."

And other partings have come: all the world's thickness lies between brother and brother—one here, one keeps his Christmas in the midsummer of the earth's other side, and quarrels and jealousies have divided those who were dear to each other once—one half-grudges the others new wealth or consequence, and one has outgrown the old friend's homeliness and mediocrity.

We must fain think of the child that was once ourself, and fain regret him; but the cure of the wounds we have put upon him lies in the little hand of the other Child; the scars in it can take out all ours.

Only the Baby in the Manger can give us back what we grown men have wasted. Let the children, and the lonely, gather Him to their chilled heart, and He will nestle to them; this thick night of self-blurred murk and freezing will hang out again its leading star, noise and jostle will pause to listen again for the carol-cry of glory and of peace, and the poverty of the sweet stable will make us rich, or heal the hunger wealth may have brought us.

The child, we said, whose circle Death has never touched, is jealous of Easter's praise for Christmas, and to him Easter seems an age away; but to us elders the Resurrection Feast comes hot-foot on the Birth Feast, and is not its rival, but its complement; our many years have broken the ring we remember, there are more gaps now than links; but a few years more and Easter will make it whole again.

The more we make our Christmas a part of our religion the less can age steal from it. It is a sad season only to them in whose mind it is but a memory of outgrown happiness—a day of contrasts. It is all too common a plaint with some that for them it is no time of mirth—an occasion rather of poignant reminders hard to face without wincing. If we could think less of ourselves and more of the Little Child who came to lead us, less of Christmas would be lost; for He is not lost, nor anything He brought. The more Christian our Christmas is, the more will its sweetness survive all time's assault: it is when we make of a great feast of our religion only a half pagan wassail-day that it fails us after youth is fled. The Child of the Manger was not to lie there a Child for ever, and the Man of the Cross knew all that we have learned of life's shadow, and can brighten it and sweeten it. It is only when we lose sight of Christmas as the first act in the drama of redemption that its joy seems to elude us as the years run by. And it is because millions do forget, that their Christmas mirth rings hollow and half-hearted, and to the sad seems heartless.

On Christmas Day, as on every other day, Death comes to many homes. Can mourners feel happy? Only if they remember that the birth of the Child at Bethlehem was the cure of Death for ever.

No man can bring back the past or call childhood back, merry and innocent; but the present is our own, and out of it we can make the future.

A few more Yules, and, if we will, we may keep our Christmas with the Master of it, and hear the same angels singing who welcomed Him to churlish Bethlehem.

PAGAN YULE

DICKENS revelled in Christmas writing as he "wallowed naked in the pathetic," and his Christmas writing makes delightful reading. So is *Bracebridge Hall* delightful and *Old-fashioned Christmas,* and no bit of writing could be more perfect in its kind than George Eliot's Christmas described in *Silas Marner.* And there are unnumbered passages in other writers that do meet homage to what Dickens calls the fine old season.

And more than half the charm in all of these is due to the season itself, whereto they serve as mirrors. To be savoured aright they must be read at Christmas: in a hot August afternoon they will be scarce more entrancing than a mince-pie. Even when enjoyed in season they suggest to the adult reader one consideration: that, to relish Christmas thus described, one had better be pretty well-off. One may even realise that a Pickwickian Christmas implies an iron constitution and an impregnable digestion. Mr. Pickwick's Christmas was, not to put too fine a point upon it, gluttonous; and if elderly gentlemen who get drunk deserve a headache in the morning Mr. Pickwick certainly deserved one.

To be of a bilious habit is, perhaps, criminal: but

no one labouring under that imperfection could have faced a Dingley Dell Christmas even with resignation.

The Christmas of our dear friend presupposes a chronic thirst, a Gargantuan appetite, and roaring spirits: and especially it implies a pocket proportionate to their indulgence. To suggest that a Dickensian Christmas is partly based on a cosy affectation would be Scroogian and horrid. Lots of folk are still young, many are wealthy, England is not yet entirely peopled by dyspeptics, in spite of the advertisements of pills and beans: and even the wicked creatures with middling taxable incomes will stretch a point and spend a little extra on Christmas jollities. God bless them all!

But, however gladly we would forget poverty and pain, anxiety and lonely sickness, they do not cease because we think it unseasonable to remember their existence. They will not be Pod-snapped away. Nothing would have shocked that immortal and still insistent personage more than to breathe a mention of them in his ear, or in that of the young person, at his well-laden Yule-night board. He would not hear of them: he waved them aside.

Can we wave them aside? Can we make them non-existent? Have old-age pensions obliterated them, or Trade Unions, or any other substitute for the peace of God?

If not, is Christmas, after all, an orgy of the rich? Are the poor and wretched to understand that their business on the feast is to be forgotten?

If it were so the reason would be, flatly, this: that Christmas has lost its Christian meaning and ossified into a pagan carnival. A day of mere gorging and extravagance can concern the poverty-stricken very little: an extra glass or so of gin on credit, by some easy-tempered landlord's indulgence, is about all they can look for to celebrate the day.

And how suggestive of wealth and feasting the Bethlehem stable is! How rich the Child there, and His Mother and her spouse!

God rest you, merry gentlemen, have a thought of that Child, poor no longer, and help the poor children and their much poorer parents. Was Dives a disreputable person? What harm did he, except that, while he ate pleasantly, there was unfed Lazarus at his gate? Did *he* bid the wretch starve? Had *he* defrauded or impoverished him?

Nay, but though every Dives in all England should forget the empty bellies, through solicitude for his own, over-weighted and outraged, yet will not Christ. It is *not* the rich man's festival: it is only his extravagant opportunity. The pauper Child, in the chill stable, it is His feast, and His gifts are for all: only they are pushed aside and unnoted.

If Christmas in England were more Christian its contrasts would not make us gasp, and half-shame us of our own well-being. Were the contrasts so ghastly in the old days before the dour Reformation came to shut the monk's guest-houses, and give to the indigent Poor Laws instead?

Let the rich do what they can—if they would—to sweeten the sting of poverty: let Christ's charity brood wider than any new-fangled State Philanthropy: and yet there will be poor, and sad, and sick. We know it well.

Is there *no* cure?

Only one: the Child Himself.

Give *Him* back to the people: teach Him again. Cease cheating the children of England of their knowledge of Him, and their share in Him, and half the bitterness of being unwillingly like Him in his penury will be healed. Go on breeding up England's children pagans, and, as they grow in numbers, so will the huge total grow of those who see in poverty the only shame and evil, the one thing intolerable.

Make your Christmas more and more heathen, be less and less mindful of its Christian meaning, and more and more will the pagan poor hate and envy and grudge the selfish, smug Christmas of the rich. Shoulder Christ out of Christmas, and a chill more bitter than that of the wintry night will benumb the hearts of rich and poor alike. In Bethlehem was no room, in home or inn, for the Divine outcast; that, not the poverty of the place, made poignant the pathos of the stable. And less and less room for Him is found in home and hostel among us: because His story is fast fading into legend—for how can He be known to a nation to whom He is not taught? The children of England are stolen from the Child: and the children become men as churlish to Him as they of Bethlehem, unwitting of His presence in their midst. Let England go on thus, breeding up heathens, and her ginshops and brothels will be full, her churches empty: the hooligan will illustrate her civilisation, and those whose bed, on Christmas night, is on the windy wall beside the cold river will witness to the fine State Philanthropy that serves our modern world in place of the Church's ancient charity. All the more bitter is their chill for that they know nothing of the Child who left Heaven for the stable: is it their fault? How *should* they know, who may be taught anything else but that?

The Reformation robbed the English poor of their Church: the new education has stolen Christ out of their lives, and ousted Him from their homes. Does the decorous statesman, listening in his highly garnished church, to the old tale of churlish Bethlehem, pause to wonder from how many doors he has helped to drive Christ into the night: how dire he has helped to make the poverty of those who were poor enough before? Sharp and biting close can be the want of the poor Christian: but how death-cold is the penury of the poor pagan who has not even learned of hope.

ONCE AGAIN

TO hear him talk you would say that Man was a self-satisfied animal, but it is only his little way: all these trumpetings are merely for the public. He remains personally unconvinced. In reality dissatisfaction comes easier to him than optimism, and his deepest dissatisfaction is commonly with his circumstances, of which he counts himself a part. Whoever else heeds his boastings, he does not: they are only an uneasy effort at self-defence, to prevent his contemporaries from arriving at his own conclusions about himself.

This is not saying that he is really a humble creature, for humility is not quite the same thing as a sense of soreness at not being a finer fellow. Humility never thinks of being fine.

Of course there are people whose optimism begins, like charity in the proverb, at home: they are impervious to experience of themselves, and judge themselves by their preconceived picture of themselves without any tedious comparisons of it with the original. Outside opinion has no weight with them, and they are never dashed by any failures to behave as they have decided that they will behave. A revelation from on high would not convince them that they were not particularly like the ideal they have very pleasantly conceived of themselves. They do not need to boast, for boasting implies a certain insincerity.

But they are, I think, rare birds: most people think worse of themselves than would appear, and are rather pessimistic in their own regard than over-sanguine. And that, perhaps, is why persons who have reached a point beyond youth shrink instinctively from the making of good resolutions.

It is a shallow assumption that the only difficulty about good resolutions is in the keeping of them; that simply to make them is as easy as admitting that two and two are four. It may be easy for the young, who have but a short experience of themselves, to damp them: who still suppose that to resolve and to do are much the same thing. But it is not such a comfortable process for those who have learned, by a hundred trials, how wide the difference is between resolving and achieving. Once bitten, twice shy: and every broken resolution leaves the mark of its teeth on us.

It is not, again, so easy to be insincere with ourselves as is commonly pretended: to arrive at anything like compete and complacent insincerity with oneself is a matter of much time and effort and implies a habit formed by innumerable pitiful acts, and much more deliberate intention than is at all usual. The majority of imperfect human creatures are not so apt to be insincere with themselves as to be pusillanimous; they are more liable to think themselves hypocritical than to be so, and of having to think themselves hypocrites they are unduly fearful. For they have not the pluck to tell themselves (and the Devil) that the good in themselves is just as real as the bad: perceiving by experience that the good has often been sent to the wall by the bad, they are ever-ready to listen when the Devil assures them that the bad was all genuine and the good a mere pretence all along. If your self-complacent, personal optimist is a rare bird, I believe your proper hypocrite to be much rarer. If he be so common as is pretended why do I not continually meet him? Ask any priest and see if he will tell you that he comes across many hypocrites. Inconsistency is not hypocrisy: to aim at a tree-top and only hit one of the lower boughs may not be marksmanship, but it is not hypocritical:

"He who means the sky
Shoots higher far than he that means a tree."

It is a shame to talk as though the poor fellow who tries a higher standard than he has grace for is a hypocrite. But no one is more ready to condemn him than himself. Deadly conscious of a thousand failures, he comes to fancy that a new attempt would be insincerity. And so he shrinks from making good resolutions; partly out of a timorous dread of his own accusation of hypocrisy, and partly out of a dismal sense of the labour it involves—a labour so often proved unfruitful. For the labour grows more and more. There is an exhilaration in the first repentance: 'tis a novel excursion into a region

full of promise.   But what broken promise is so
bitter to remember as our own?   It is only in childhood that the broken promises of other people hurt
and surprise us much: they cease to scandalise us
as we grow older: but our own promises broken hurt
and horrify us still.   So we become afraid of making
them: and most of all afraid of promising to be what
we have never been.

Experientia docet, says a proverb; and like all
proverbs it is a sort of oracle; and in all oracles
there is apt to lurk a lie twisted in and out of its
truth.   Experience teaches; but does it always teach
the bravest truth?   What had experience taught
the man by the pool in Siloam through eight and
thirty gibing years?   That it was all no use: that
to-day must repeat yesterday's failure: he never *had*
had anyone help him to the healing pool, and he had
not yet: others had always had their helpers, and
they reached the saving water, and would this time
too.   But he would not listen to the cold, grim
warning of experience.   He would not heed the grin
of any looker-on: he had been trying to scramble to
the pool for thirty and eight years, and the only
hope he had was to try and scramble still.   So the
other Man came by, Who had seen each daily fruit-
less effort, and never scoffed at it, and the horrible
long patience was all forgotten.   The frouzy bed
on which he had lain so many days, wet with
tears of a thousand disappointments, the Man bade
him take up—and walk.   He never whined that he
could not: that there he must lie rotting to the

obvious end. The Kindest Voice that has ever spoken had told him to brush aside all ghastly experience, and the meaning of the Voice was Hope: as it is to all of us, who know not whither else to turn for it. Let him heed nothing but the mandate; let him stand up and look Him in the face who with such plain mercy said that he must lie on the dull reminder of his helplessness no more, but carry it away thence, and walk.

There is no other Voice that can hearten us weary with a life-time of daily failures. Our own falters: the crooked finger of our fellows points at the squalid past. Only the Faultless bids us cease to sit glowering in our faults: "Have they," He asks us gently, "abolished *Me*?"

Was it a faultless world He came to re-fashion? We are so timid that we hold ourselves as though our broken promises voided His: as if our mean experience of ourselves were to set His measure of dealing with us. Having blurred the given likeness of ourselves to Him, we forget what He is like: and obscure Him in impatience like our own, and fancy Him pitiless as our human judges are, with a stone in His fist for us like theirs.

So we shrink back, with cowardly pride, from even the worn effort to be different: as if a new year could hold for us no hope stouter than the years already wasted. Because our hope has been in our-selves, and we are so bitter slow to learn that it can only be in Him.

GOODBYE—AND WELCOME

NINETEEN HUNDRED AND THIR-TEEN is on his last legs, and in a few days they will have carried him off, with all his imperfections on his head, to stand for judgment among all the other past things and years.

He came into the world weighted with the heavy disadvantage of a bad name: the people who bother themselves and their neighbours about "luck," never expected any good of him; and every evil that befell any of us during his course was no matter of surprise to *them*.

"What else could you look for in the year '13?" they demanded with a grizzly complacence. Well, they may comfort themselves with the reflection that 2013 can do *them* no harm.

It is not pretty, anyway, to insult a death-bed, and it is not our intention now to repeat the tale of offences chargeable by the human race against 1913; and old folk are argumentative—he might pretend that some of the trouble was of man's own making as much as his. If, he might urge, you men would be less greedy, less quarrelsome, less vindictive, less furiously hurried, more deliberate, more patient, more charitable to each other, a little wiser, and a little more mutually considerate among yourselves,

I might have been as lucky a year as the rest. Meanwhile, I want to repent of my real faults, and you may as well make the responses to my Litany of self-condemnation.

I suppose the years also suffer a particular as well as a general judgment; only that the former, in their case, is often crude and hasty, and is liable to considerable revision by the latter. So, all we need do, is to call out to our unpopular friend, 1913, as he goes, "Goodbye—and Welcome." Should he be sensitive to innuendo he may scent one in the form of the farewell, though we, of course, mean only, "And welcome 1914."

When we watch other friends leaving us we know that they take with them something of our own—a bit of our heart at least, and perhaps other trifles. A parting year cannot go empty-handed either; three score and ten are the golden coins life is apt to promise us for our spending, and one of them (whether our stock be really seventy or no) he carries off in his fist. What has he left us for it? Nay, what did we buy with it? A better conscience, a higher purpose; some translation of fine purpose into decent achievement; some lesson learned; some ugly knowledge unlearned; a gentle patience; a more patient hope?

There is only One who can answer, and He will not—yet.

It is no wonder, says the Autocrat of the Breakfast Table, that when two men talk to each other they are so liable to misunderstand—six folk all speaking at once! "Six?" demanded, I think, the young man called John.

"Why, yes," answered the Autocrat (I quote only his substance, out of a naughty memory). "Take Tom and Bill. There's Tom as Bill thinks he is, and Tom as Tom thinks he is, and Tom as God knows him to be: and Bill as Tom imagines him, and Bill as Bill imagines himself, and Bill as God knows he is: all at loggerheads."

And out of all those six, there's only one on each side that matters. The world may think that you have done a lot in 1913, and you may think you have done worse than nothing: the fact does not lie somewhere between the world and you, but up in heaven, where God knows.

To me it seems a comfortable truth: the world is no pattern of perfection, but God save us from its judgment: only to the judgment of Perfection can Imperfection look with any hope. Who, if God would suffer it, would choose that the final judgment should be passed on himself, by himself? "For though our heart reprehend us, God is greater than our heart, and knoweth all things." So wrote the Beloved of Love itself, echoing something he had overheard from the Heart whereby he lay that last supper-night before the King put on His Crown, and mounted his bitter throne to reign in sweetness.

Repentance is our self-function not judgment. That is no more ours than it is our fellow-man's: "Neither judge I myself," said St. Paul. We are know-nothings, and our Hope must stretch out pleading fingers to Omniscience—only another name of His who called Himself Charity.   And He tells us what it means.   "Charity is patient, is kind . . . seeketh not her own, is not provoked to anger, thinketh no evil, rejoiceth not in iniquity, endureth all things.   Charity never falleth away . . . we know in part . . ."

But Charity is Omniscience, and greater than our heart, and knoweth all things.

Of God's patience and compassion we all take account when it is question of great sinners—has He no patience or compassion for those who try not to sin, and fail, and go on trying?   When we are mad with impatience against ourselves, and our failures and sloth, is it out of humility?   "He who believeth, let him not make haste."   Was Isaias giving a Counsel of Imperfection—or remembering that we must go up step by step, and that the steps are steep, and our knees faltering, and only by the Hand of Omnipotent Charity can we be helped and heartened up at all?

1913 is not our judge; only one of many witnesses. Another witness is coming; neither in *his* eyes can we throw dust; he comes not really to give or to steal, but to watch.   He shall invent nothing, foist up no slander against us, but note what he sees.   It depends on us, and whether we let God help us, or shoulder Him away from our lives.

We need not too tediously wander back over the dull, stubbled fields of the dead year to scan if there be, after all, some forgotten gleanings of good grain

belonging to us: God will do that for us, did it when
we were not looking. A father's tenderness does not
ignore the good points in his worst son: they never
slip *his* memory. Eh! What things God makes
much of—half a soldier-lad's cloak to make him
warm in Heaven, Who had all the universe of stars
for the fringe of His raiment.

"Little Brothers," pleaded the Poor Man of
Assisi, with a patience and modesty learnt out of the
Heart of the Poor Man of Nazareth, "let us begin
to love Jesus Christ a little."

It is high time. Where have we been all these
truant years; what silly, ugly things have we been
teaching ourselves were wise and fine, outside the
school where the humble Master has been asking,
asking that the three and thirty letters of his
alphabet might spell for us the only word we need
—Love? Birth and Death, Miracle and Parable,
the long, silent years after Bethlehem and before
Calvary, Pity and Patience, Healing and Help, His
daily toil for His daily bread, all the thirty and
three letters that made that Life on earth of the
Carpenter whose Throne the angels were bowing
down before in Heaven. He keeps his patient eyes
on us, pushing them to us this way and that, and
bids us group them into one word: what *can* they
spell but Love?

Can the angels understand? All their knowledge is not Omniscience, and its light makes even
their science cast a shadow; and all along they have

been watching Him and us. Can they understand
it, Divine Patience and human refusal? They saw
the Child when first He came at Bethlehem; watched
His exiled babyhood, His ignored childhood; heard
Joseph command, and saw Him obey; hovered about
His work, as He learned it; listened when He began
at last to teach, and missed no miracle He did, up
to the last miracle of His raising Himself from
death. Alas, they saw us too: saw our first
repulse of Him at Bethlehem, hardily maintained
ever since: that He came to His own, and His own
received Him not they knew before St. John put it
into piteous words, and the world is His own as
much as ever, and will no more receive Him now
than at first. Can they fathom it? They know
who He is, and what we are; and they have to stand
by and watch Him standing, a beggar for love,
showing His wounds at the gate of the hearts of
men, outside. Cold was the night wind when He
came, colder and colder blows the blast of man's
indifference, in which mankind itself is freezing to
death. And they see it all; men huddled and
grovelled at the feet of any tyrant, lying and cruel;
blind with staring at any beauty that is scarce at
pains to hide its ugliness and horror behind a half-
mask—but resolute to defend themselves against the
King who will not call us servants, but friends, and
with eyes obstinately shut against the loveliness of
the Most Beautiful of the children of men.

Quamdiu? How long, they must needs cry out,

will the incomprehensible story last; when shall God write *Finis* to the book of His long patience and of man's thankless insolence?

Meanwhile they come to each of us, the escort to every man of another year; and they whisper, with shamed angelic faces, let *this* hold your Reparation: let it make up for the stale failures of the past, and carry through its length message after message of awakening tenderness. *Abyssus abyssum invocat*— the fathomless deeps of God's love cry out to you to deepen your heart for Him: till at last you, knowing that all your fault and failure is known, may still gather hope because you also can cry:

"But, Lord Thou knowest all things, Thou knowest that I love thee."

OF CAMEL SWALLOWING

THE Eighteenth Century, which had amassed a good deal that was especially its own to leave, apart from what it had inherited, bequeathed to its posterity, among other things, an intense dislike of miracles. That dislike was partly an heirloom, neatly conserved in Protestant wrappings, rather yellow and cracked at the joints; but eighteenth century attachment to Protestantism was mainly negative—it did not so much love Protestantism for what it had modestly represented itself to be, as liked it for certainly not being something else. Protestantism, wherever it was, had always announced itself as Christianity Pure and Evangelical, and the Eighteenth Century was not particularly fond of Christianity at all; but, then, Protestantism was obviously not Catholicity, and that was everything. In so far as Protestantism had got rid of the Pope, and of Papal Dogma, it was truly admirable; in so far as it retained a belief in Christianity, as a religion implying faith in Christ as God, it had much to learn of the negative kind, of the Eighteenth Century; and it did not obstinately refuse to be taught.

Thus, the heirloom we have mentioned, carefully

treasured by the Eighteenth Century, was handed on with a new, or somewhat enlarged, purpose.

The original and traditional Protestant objection to miracles made a distinction; it had been largely due to the fact that for many hundreds of years the miracles had been Catholic miracles, and to admit them would have been incompatible with the simple theory that the Pope was Antichrist. All the miracles, during all the ages, in which the performers were compelled to confess that the Papal Church had existed, were redolent of a Catholic taint; they had been the indiscreet work of saints indubitably Catholic and Papal, or had been connected with some distinctively Catholic doctrine, such as the belief in Holy Relics (as of the True Cross, or the other instruments of the Passion,) and the belief in the Real Presence of Christ in the Eucharist. If such miracles had been true, it would, the Reformers perceived, be difficult to maintain that the religion they had illustrated was false and abominable to God. But there had been, said, they, an earlier age, when there was no Church in the Papal sense of it; a pure, Biblical, unecclesiastical age, when bishops were merely Presbyterian ministers with large congregations. Miracles in that age were on a different footing; instead of offensively arguing in favor of a haughty Papal Church, they would only be a proof of the divine sanctions of Christianity—pure New Testament Christianity. (St. Stephen and St. James of Jerusalem were unhappily not New Testament Christians, as no part of the New Testament had been written while they were alive.) So "Bible" miracles were all right, and, for much the same reason, "Ecclesiastical" miracles were all wrong.

The Eighteenth Century, however, was not wrapped up in the New Testament, and was, indeed, remarkably disengaged as to the Divine origin, basis, and authority of Christianity. So it handed on the miracle-hating heirloom with an added gusto, and without any reservations. For many ages miracles had done a pestilent work in confirming the belief of a credulous world in the supernatural character and Divinely accredited Mission of the Papal Church: that was pitiable and shocking. But to retain belief in *any* miracles, even though reported in the New Testament, would only tend to maintain the hideous shackles of "superstition," that is, of the foolish idea that Christianity itself was anything more than a growth—like the inimitable British Constitution; that it was, in fact, a supernatural religion, with a supernatural origin, a Divine Founder, a Divine Revelation, and a Divine (instead of a merely political, ethical and utilitarian) Authority and Mission. The strong and determined preoccupation of the Eighteenth Century was to escape altogether from the incubus of the supernatural; religion could only be tolerated as a Department of State, like the Lunacy Board, and few things could be imagined more inconvenient and embarrassing than a State Department with a Divine and irresponsible head. "What constitution," as the doctor argued against

Eternal Punishment, "could stand it?" Some Eighteenth Century legacies have been lost or dissipated. There are people who think the present age less well-mannered, and less addicted to books, more frankly superficial, and more frankly greedy. But the dislike of miracles is still much prized.

The grounds of a survival that might seem archaic, the reasons for this antipathy, are worth conjecturing. The explanation cannot be found in "the fact that miracles are impossible." Nothing is more attractive to contemporary taste (so to speak) than the obviously and demonstrably impossible. Write a novel hanging on an "impossible fact," and it's odd if it be ever popular, *experto crede;* tell a story, at a dinner party, involving two or three physical impossibilities, and you will be asked again; tell another, with twenty points each irreconcilable with Euclid or the late Professor Huxley, and you will have invitations for an entire season.

It is not because the present age is overridden by logic, or by its profound realization of, and reverence for, admitted discoveries in the realm of science (where nothing but what is physical may dare to assert its existence), that it can't stand a miracle. I dare say that nine agnostic metaphysicians out of ten would handsomely admit that a Jesuit is likely to be as good a logician as a stockbroker, and that ninety-nine physicists out of a hundred would freely confess that the laws of physics are not even darkly surmised by that omniscience classically termed the Man in the Street.

But the man in the street is too wide-awake for a miracle. Why? Because the rules of evidence are better realized by him than they were, for instance, by St. Thomas Aquinas. Not precisely; the only rules of evidence he studies are those illustrated in criminal trials, his greedy, ghoulish and obscene taste for which is pandered to by the most indecent press that ever existed, a press whose hero is the murderer, and whose heroine is the adulteress.

But from the man in the street belief in the supernatural has been sedulously eliminated. If miracles were merely vulgar stupidities, or dark and foul abnormalities, he would swallow them voraciously; and his press would pry his mouth open, if he was not already agape for them, that they might be pushed in and down with the least attempt at discussion or mastication.

"Ecclesiastical" miracles stand on a different base, and are evidences of life and action in a higher plane; they presuppose God, as a saint presupposes God. Saints are the world's fools as they are God's wise men. And miracles are intolerable to a society that wants to forget God, because their occurrence is an insistence on Him; they are an insuperable reminder that human life is not a sheer anarchy, though it may be in a wide-spread rebellion against an Omnipotent Master: for every miracle, by the essential fact that it is a suspension of, or an exception to law, proves the law, and insists on the Lawgiver who alone can override it. A miracle is explicable only on one hypothesis, that God exists and is Om-

nipotent. So the man who is only sure of one thing
—that belief in God, His law, and His omnipotent
justice, that must reward or punish, is inconvenient
to him—will jeer at every miracle suggested, apart
altogether from the question of evidence; but he
will listen, greedily, to a tale that is not explicable
on any hypothesis whatever. To hear of impossibilities delights his craving for what is unreal, feeds
his morbid appetite for the flatly incomprehensible,
and releases him, he fancies, for a moment from that
dull prison of hideous materialism in which by his
own choice he is bound; he knows how vulgar and
sordid his gaol is, and he wistfully turns to avenues
of escape more vulgar and sordid still. His own experiences have been mostly all commonplace, and
such as any dull and unscrupulous animal might
share with him; he devours hungrily the experiences
alleged by some one else that range into the unfet-
tered regions of blank impossibility. But a miracle!
That is not impossible, not incomprehensible either,
if God be remembered, and His Omnipotence realized; only he does not at all wish to remember God,
and Omnipotent Justice is a bleak thing to contrast
with certain habits of his own. Those other impossibilities have no ethical significance whatever,
and the tales of them are free from that tedious
thing, a moral; that is what is so nice about them.
If Jones, as Smith avers, patted Smith's shoulder in
Piccadilly, on a date specified, and took him into a
pastry cook's to eat ices (of which he had ever been
inordinately fond), and it subsequently transpired

that poor Jones was, at that identical moment, being himself devoured by a tiger (also notoriously addicted to this sort of refreshment) in Bengal—it is enthrallingly interesting, and does not in the least imply that Williams need lead a better life. There is nothing personal about that camel, and Williams swallows it with ease and pleasure, unconcerned by the odd appearance it may lend to his figure. But a miracle, once taken into the system would logically imply consequences: God; a moral law not identical with that of the clubs; obedience, or disobedience— with results. An inconvenient gnat that. A regular diet of camels leads nowhere—there's the beauty of it—whereas a single miracle admitted into, and lodged in, the system may demand a total change of life and habits. All the Williamses, a "practical" race, members of the best clubs, and immovably resolved to lose no pleasure, no profit, and no advantage in the gift of World, Flesh or Devil, naturally choke at the mere sight of a gnat, and naturally prefer being camel-swallowers.

TASTE AND TOLERANCE

IS not the simple truth this—that there may profitably be as many different sorts of sermons as there are different sorts of people? And is not the frank recognition of this very simple truth a legitimate encouragement to different sorts of preachers? Some who are bound to preach are thoroughly aware that they are not what is called good preachers; for the sake of those who are their listeners they wish they were; and for their own sake too, since it is human nature to desire that any work we have to do should not be of an inferior quality. Nevertheless it does not follow that the defect of preaching power they admit in themselves, and regret, even when others would agree with their self-criticism, is in actual reality so serious a drawback as it would superficially appear. A priest may be, as he humbly conceives, a "bad preacher," and it is likely enough that there will be critics to remark it: but there is more in a man than anything he says, and that superiority of the man himself to his words is not lost in the pulpit. Indeed, it is often to the *man* we listen rather than to any special things he may enunciate in speech. His congregation knows him for a good man, and it matters more to them than his phrases or epithets. The phrases may lack

much; they may be somewhat flat, somewhat outworn; they may be very inadequate to the nobility
of his theme, poorly inexpressive of sublime ideas,
miserably weak for the weight of the message intended: his use of epithets may be even tedious; he
chooses them awkwardly, and they may be, and often
are, calculated rather to dull the force of what he
means than to sharpen and illustrate it. But none
of this matters so much as he, meekly aware of it
all, though helpless to better it, imagines: because
the force is in himself that he, and others too, miss
in his words.

He may dutifully spend all the hours available in
preparation, and the result almost disheartens him:
but the real preparation has been in his life, and the
result does not depend on his present, conscious effort.

Of course a congregation likes "good sermons";
enjoys them, and perhaps may remember them better than "bad sermons"; it may grumble at the "bad"
sermons: nevertheless it profits by them, by reason
of the man himself. For the only really bad sermons would be such as were insincere. A platitude
in the pulpit is not a stale saying, but a saying which
is only words and has no conviction at the back of
it.

Say a sermon was "stupid." It does not follow it
is bad. It may be thoroughly earnest, but the
thoughts are, perhaps, dull and pedestrian. A congregation is, as our old grammars would say, a
noun of multitude, and in a multitude there are many

people: some are neither dull nor stupid, their thoughts are not precisely pedestrian: well, they are bored. They are disposed to think the sermon beneath them. Let them practise patience and humility. But in the congregation are some dull folk too, honest creatures, and the honest stupid sermon suits them. It is their turn to be satisfied. The finer discourses, though just as honest and sincere, are over their heads, and they would be bored too if they dared.

A sermon which is insincere expresses nothing, however big the words: it is the only bad sort, and is worst of all for the preacher.

The fact, not a recondite one, of there being so many different kinds of people in even an average congregation of no uncommon size, makes part of the preacher's difficulty. He would wish to be of use to all, but he cannot even know what all need, even if, knowing, he were able to give each what was especially useful to each. But some difficulties are so great that they answer themselves: God asks none of us to do impossibilities, and He asks no one to do two things at once. It is we ourselves, who try, if we be over-solicitous, and unconsciously fussed by expecting too much of ourselves. It is very right we should do our best, and not let ourselves off with less: but our best is not always equally good, and if somebody else's worst is better than our best it is not his fault, and need not be our misfortune. It is a lucky stone that kills two birds at one throw; we need not worry ourselves if in one sermon we cannot take direct aim at two or three hundred birds at once. After all, the plain truth, if we stick to it, hits everybody, and if it hits many who have been hit before, it is all right: the truest truths are not the newest.

Though nine-tenths of a congregation should go away and think we had made no great figure, they do not know all about it. God does, and He does not specially care for majorities. Even if only one person has got any good of us, and we cannot know of even that one, God is not necessarily dissatisfied. We do not read of flocks of converts after the Sermon on the Mount, and it *was* the Sermon on the Mount, and God preached it. After the Crucifixion itself, after the Resurrection, the number of those He had converted, in three and thirty years, appears to have been about a hundred and twenty. What do we expect?

To return to the variousness of hearers: surely it leaves us ground for hoping that all sorts of sermons may appeal to some.

It may well be that a greater number will prefer the style that is called popular. It may well be admitted, too, that there is more than mere preference: that the "popular" sermon not only pleases, but profits them best. They cannot attend without interest, and only this sort awakes their interest. Their emotions want stirring: without emotion they are dead, and nothing arouses their emotion but the downright "popular" sermon. It would be affectation to ignore that emotion is a large part of us, and it is utterly unfair to pretend that there is anything inferior in appeal to emotion in preaching.   No other road is open to the interior of immense numbers of people: why should we leave the devil the key of the gate?   If we occupy the path there is the less room for the three concupis-cences to lodge in it.

Let us be plain-spoken: there are huge numbers who can hardly be awaked from spiritual somnolence and lethargy except by a method of preaching that is, not to put too fine a point upon it, ranting.   Then let those who can rant.   It is not the highest style of preaching?   Never mind, if it catches lower-class souls.   A silken net never caught a whale—his blubber weighs too much.   To tell the truth it is not a net that does catch him, but harpoons, 'and there is blood about while the harpooning is going forward.

St. Paul, we may be reminded, never ranted. For my part I do not know, for I never heard.   But of one thing we may feel quite sure, he would have used any sort of sermon that his unfailing spiritual instinct showed him was called for by the quality of his audience.   If there be listeners who in spiritual matters are semi-deaf, and you can shout, then shout.   It others can hear only partly with their ears, and have to listen with their eyes as well; then jump about.   Only shout the truth: no yelling will make two and two more than four: and do not lash yourself into an excitement that you do not feel; if a genuine fervor jumps you, never mind how

high; but, for shame's sake, do not try and skip
yourself above yourself or your sincere emotion.
Even that might bring you popularity, but there is
One among your audience who will not away with it.
Anything else He will suffer; slips of grammar,
faults of "taste," indifferent arguments, two-legged
syllogisms, lapses of memory, historical blunders,
controversial insecurity, *argumenta ad homines
etiam imbecilles,* but not that: nor *stage* violence;
the stage-hero, denouncing the stage-villain does
not, for all his rage, think a penny the worse of him:
they are the best of friends and will sup together
presently. Though he foam with rage at the mouth,
no one supposes him to be in the least angry; no one
wants him to be. His voice may crack with the fury
of his tirade against the monster opposite, but it
would not scandalize us to hear of his borrowing ten
shillings from the monster before they part for the
night. On the stage neither hero nor villain speaks
his *own* feelings, for himself, but the feelings of his
part: the villain may be the hero in to-morrow's
play: and no one will think he has morally degener-
ated: the villain takes the character of persecuted
merit and he is not pretending to be a jot better than
he was yesterday. He is deceiving nobody, and trying to deceive nobody. Stage acting is not pretence.
But I should be pretending were I in the pulpit to
assume a fire that had not set me alight, in hopes that
it might enkindle me. The actor is guilty of no insincerity: he is only trying to express another man's
sentiment with all the force he can summon: I should

be guilty of the worst sort of insincerity trying to deceive myself first that others might be deceived the more defencelessly. *Non sic ad astra.*

This is not saying that a preacher is not to be warmed by his theme: the more it heats him the more likelihood that others will be set on fire. By all means let his theme warm him: only let it be that: let the theme do it, not himself. It can only be from sincere enthusiasm that a man is genuinely carried way. But there may be a pulpit excitement which is not the irresistible effect of genuine enthusiasm. It may be "effective", but it effects nothing for God. Not by making folk stare can we force the Spirit of God to come down into them. I dare say there were many on Carmel who thought it a fine thing when Baal's priests cried out and cut themselves with knives after their manner, but it brought no fire down from heaven.

It is supercilious and pharisaic to decry preaching because it is emotional. Is it pretended that our emotions were all given us by Satan? He certainly aims at getting hold of them: why should not we pre-occupy them for God? Only let the emotion be honest, and genuine; nothing *real* is useless. It is not to the point to urge that emotion is transient. Life itself is transient. Any emotion we feel may be our last; it must be better that it should be an emotion on God's side. The chances are, as we say in common speech, it will. *not* be our last. Admit it dies down: still it has grooved a mark on our soul, and a good one. Say it is a fire gone out: it may

well leave a smouldering spark capable of re-kind-
ling: when a fire is gone out, all is not instantly
cold. Put it at its worst: the flame is extinguished,
the heat is chilled: still there *was* fire and good fire.
It is better to have been hot on God's side for a
time than to have been cold throughout. A thing
which is not the very best must be far better than the
worst of all: and the worst thing of all is complacent,
unmoved spiritual lethargy: it is the beginning of a
habit and tends to be a fixed one: once fixed, not
sermons but miracles are needed to break up that
ever-thickening ice.

If I labour this it is lest any reader should think
me *against* preaching of the popular, vehement kind:
there are many who need it: let us confess it again,
many who need downright "ranting," in which there
may be more sentiment than thought, for many
have much less capacity for thinking than they have
for feeling: and no preaching can confer a capacity
that is wanting: a preacher, indeed, may be capable
of *educating* dormant capacity, but hardly in one
sermon, and he may have only the opportunity of
one: he does what he can with the material on which
he has to work that once.

An audience may be thoroughly unintellectual and
not in the least vulgar. But it may even be vulgar.
Yet vulgar men and women have souls, and they are
not a bit more easy to save on that account. They
also need preaching, and if any will sink himself to
them it is a great work. It may be to the preacher
a great mortification too: one from which some-

thing within him shrinks as something in a saint shrank when he put his lips to a sore. Not all of us could do what St. Catherine did at Siena, what St. Ignatius did: we are not saints. But if a man will do even that for Christ, it *must* bear fruit: it was only when Catherine drank her awful cup that the nearly lost soul of Andrea was won. And ou Lord made the ghastly drink sweet.

If a preacher should bend his head to catch souls even through the vulgarity of their ears, let us be content to confess that we could not do it ourselves, and stand aside for him. God knows: and He does not ask us to do what we cannot do. When we know He asks us to do something, then we know that we can do it, though we have thought it a moral impossibility, or a physical: it is a physical impossibility for a man with a withered hand to stretch it out; but He bade the man stretch it out and he did, else would he have carried it withered to the grave.

What we cannot do ourselves let us not refuse leave to others to do, in preaching also. There is room for all sorts.

But just as in a congregation there may be some whom, humanly speaking, a preacher can reach only by rhetoric, fine rhetoric; or by a rhetoric less fine, if more fiery; or by vehemence; or even by a rough wit, and banter (as one may often hear in a Catholic country); so there are others to whom even fine rhetoric in a pulpit is almost repugnant; to whom a rhetoric that fails of being fine, and is only fierce, is utterly repugnant; to whom any extreme vehemence is repellent and physically disagreeable, and well-night intolerable; whom the heat of some preachers does not warm but chill, with a quite involuntary sense of shrinking, almost of aversion, almost of protest. They are as unaffected in disliking violent action, noisy declamation, passionate appeal to emotion, as those who like it are sincere in admiration. It does not carry them off their legs, but stiffens their backs. It does not engage their sympathy, but arouses a perfectly genuine remonstrance, and goes far to awaken an antipathy that they can no more help than they can help preferring argument to assertion, and proof to argument. It is no more conceited in them to have one sort of taste than it is beggarly and mean in others to have a different taste, or no taste at all. In the one case the popular preacher appeals to a natural quality of mind; in the other the natural quality of mind is all against such an appeal as his. They are not to condemn *him;* but neither are they bound in sincerity to condemn themselves. If they should belittle him, and deny *him* sincerity, they misbehave: but it is not misbehavior in them not to like what the tone of their mind dislikes. If they are wishing it was a different sort of preacher's turn to hold the pulpit, they are only yielding to the same spontaneous feeling as the man in the next pew who is rejoicing that he came to-night instead of to-morrow—to-morrow when the vault will resound with no loud echoes, and a very quiet voice will lay down, in measured cadence, positions from which there is no logical escape: when

un-faith will be beaten with a cold rod of iron, and
unbelief be made to show itself as not only cruel
and unhappy but silly too: when humanistic excuses
for lax morals will be forced to appear no better
than vapid sentimentality, scrambling on one knock-
kneed leg. The man who loves the popular
preacher, and is only *capable* of him, is hardly to be
accused of resisting the Holy Ghost because he
merely suffers from distraction while those calm,
though really irresistible, things are being said. It
is not malice, but incapacity, that makes him think
the theologian dull. If he finds the preacher's huge
nose queer, he does not mean to be flippant: he is
only what he is, and he cannot help it. But neither is
the other man resisting the Holy Ghost because he
cannot, for the life of him, understand why rivers of
sweat should accompany allusion to the river of life
and grace. He does not *want* to be bored: he is not
assuring himself that it is superior to remain quite
cool while the preacher is so frightfully hot.
Nevertheless his mind wanders: the preacher sets it
off: the preacher starts down an alley and the
listener goes down to the end of it, while
the preacher has dashed eagerly off into another.
The preacher gives a smack at one objection to
faith, but by no means knocks it down; another has
leapt into his mind and he *must* punch at it; the listener lingers to consider how the first ought to have
been flattened; before he had made up his mind, he
sees the preacher sparring with indomitable pluck at
a third objection, with glorious pluck, but with lam-

entable want of science. Such agility makes the
hearer blink, but it is quite as fatiguing to try and
follow as it is dazzling. "Come along," cries the
preacher, with amazing spirit. "Any amount of
you. The more the merrier. I've a black eye in
my fist for each of you." The courage, the activity,
the readiness to duck, and hit, and lunge out in
another direction, are all marvellous: but a black eye
blinds no one permanently: science will give it
against the hitter for all his popularity: and this
unfortunate spectator is on the side of science, he
cares more for victory than for a fine show.

Well, well! What metaphors have we been slip-
ping into! Misfortune brings us strange bed-
fellows, says the proverb, and metaphor leads us
into odd company. I apologize, and resume.

Talking of metaphor; there may be hundreds of
profiting listeners to a rough-and-ready preacher
who have no objection in life to a mixed metaphor.
But it tries the other sort of listener. He has nothing to urge against the metaphor of shipwreck: like
the young lady in *Pride and Prejudice* who said, "The
idea of the olive-branch perhaps is not wholly new,"
he confesses to himself that the shipwreck simile is
rather venerable than original; but it is none the
less true for being time-worn. He listens with
respect; but when the preacher, hastily remembering
what is the symbol of Hope, adjures his hearers to
cling to the sheet anchor of Hope, when all is storm
and darkness, and all seem sinking, *he* cannot help
considering the buoyancy of anchors. He recognizes

that the tangled mazes of a forest brake, with thorny undergrowth, and light obscured overhead, not inaptly illustrate muddled doubt; and faith is doubt's contrary and cure; but is "faith's golden key" suggested? Are keys, even of gold, of much service to lost and benighted wayfarers?

There are, we have said, many in a given audience who can be reached by the way of feeling, and very little by appeal to thought: the avenue to their spiritual sense is the heart, and not the head. Why should we not own it, and act upon it?

But it is mainly by way of the head others are taken. Must we not acknowledge that also? No one wants to compare them or weigh their values. But facts are facts: and one of these facts is as real and legitimate as the other. Some sermons are little theological treatises, and some hearers find them heavy of digestion: not every one can assimilate the solidest food. But to some they are the most welcome kind of sermon, and not to priests only. They would as lief have their bread without sweetening or plums in it.

I heard a couple of country folk discuss a sermon once.

" 'Twere fine!" declared one. "As full of flav'rin' and fruit as a Simnel cake."

"Eh, but I've no stomach for cake," confessed the other. "I like them bready." Much more accomplished judges like them bready too.

It is objected to some preachers that they can only preach essays, and yet some people like essays, and can remember what is in them better than a more "appealing" sermon. I cannot help suspecting that some of the finest sermons we have are liable to this reproach: St. Gregory's, for example; though Cardinal Newman's are more undeniable instances. They are better printed than spoken, it may be urged. We, who only read them, and could not have heard them, cannot disprove the assertion. But it is certain that they were heard eagerly, that they drew willing throngs, and were powerfully effective: they could not have been condemned as ineffective though they had not survived their original utterance and come to be printed. Nor is it fair to urge that they were essays by essayists of extraordinary power, and therefore cannot be instanced to make a rule, as preachers of extraordinary power can never be of ordinary occurrence. Preachers of exceptional force in the other class, the class most unlike essay preachers, are of exceptional occurrence too. We do not daily fall in with the best of any sort.

What is pleaded here is that there should be no attempt to form a rule at all. That we should recognize the enormous variety of hearers, the huge divergence of taste: and frankly confess that every kind of preaching is legitimate because every kind will find some one to whom it appeals—even essay preachers.

The answer it not that a preacher must try so to modify himself as to appeal to all: he never can. He can only be himself, and the effort to be several people will not give him three heads: it was only Cerberus who, as Mrs. Malaprop said, was "three gentlemen at once."

Every preacher may not exactly suit every congregation: but it does not follow that it is the preacher's fault, any more than it is the fault of the congregation: it is nobody's fault. But I suspect that every *genuine* preacher, and we have concern with no other, suits some part of his congregation—even the essay preacher. If the congregation that does not like essays is the larger part, it is certainly their misfortune; but, majorities do so well for themselves in most ways, that, if the minority has the best of it in this instance, no frightful injustice is done. Even majorities may learn patience and be none the worse for it. If they also learned humility it would be a valuable illustration of the truth that the age of miracles is not past.

In England the finest preacher we have reads his sermons from a manuscript, and I dare say many would say they were homilies or essays. It is possible that many preachers are preferred to him by many hearers. No one wants to compel these many to hear him instead of those they prefer. But those who prefer to hear him never forget what they have heard: may they not also have their taste? It is certainly a strong measure to read a sermon from writing: it is not suggested that every preacher, or many preachers, should do it. But it might be suggested that if some preachers were to commit their sermons to writing they would never be preached—and that would be a pity, for they are excellent in their sort: only there are other sorts.

A certain Scotch minister, departing from this life, bequeathed his sermons, the sermons of forty years, to his parish. After the funeral it was debated in full *sederunt* what should be done with them. Some Elders proposed printing, others concurred, but advised selection. Finally one Elder arose and pawkily suggested that the Kirk Session should "reeverently burn them." I know one preacher, at all events, who if he should be forced to write his sermons (and read them afterward) would undoubtedly burn them—but I am not sure about "reeverently."

It is urged against the essay preachers that they are thinking of how the sermons would print. The force of the insinuation, and a real force too where the insinuation is justified, is that they are thinking not of their congregation but of the public. "Every woman writer," said Heine, "writes with one eye on herself, and one eye on some man, except Countess Hahn-Hahn, who has only one eye." If an essay preacher composes his sermons with one eye on the public and one eye on himself, he degrades the office of preaching: but he may, as well as the "popular" preacher, have both eyes on God. And truth, logic, and dogma will always "print."

ANOTHER TOLERANCE

THERE are, at the present moment, on both sides of the Atlantic, a considerable number of Catholic writers of weight whose pens are employed on works in the various departments of theology, dialectic, history, biography, and fiction, distinctly and unmistakably on the Catholic side. But there are also a number of writers, especially in the field of fiction, who are themselves Catholics but whose writing is, so to speak, non-committal. Only those who know they are Catholics *would* know they were Catholics. I would like at once to make it clear that, in so speaking of them, there is no wish on my part to find fault, or to put them on their defence. For I am not here speaking of writers who, in spite of being Catholics, write in a fashion disloyal to their religion, or injurious to it, or unworthy of it.

Reference is intended only to writers who, being Catholics, have for their theme subjects in which, they would frankly say, the question of religion does not accrue. They may be comic writers, or nursery-rhymesters, writers of fairy-tales, or novelists of the light and airy description. They may be employed in the production of short stories for the non-Catholic press, or reviewers of books for non-Catholic papers.

My object here is not to belittle them, or pick holes in their way of earning a very precarious livelihood, but, on the contrary, to put in a plea for them, and to show, if I can, that they may also do a good work. The whole question of literature and the press is one of the most important with which the Church has to concern herself in the modern world: and to that fact the rulers of the Church, not only in her metropolis, but in every country are keenly alive.

The point I would desire to accentuate is a very simple one, and perhaps may appear to be over-obvious: but it is not commonly admitted as such. And in two words, it is this: that service may be done to the good cause in many degrees of varying importance, but that even the least seemingly important is worth while and should not be decried.

Every Catholic perceives that he who writes works of Catholic theology, controversy, devotion, hagiology, history, biography, and such like, is serving the Church. So he is, and in a specially direct and unmistakable fashion.

Catholics recognize that those are serving the Church who write only fiction when the works produced by them are, in fact, works of Catholic apologetic: novels with a purpose—the obvious purpose being the presentment of the Catholic Church and faith in colors such as must recommend both to the non-Catholic reader. But in this

particular matter I venture to think that Catholics
are sometimes more eager than discreet. For I
cannot help thinking that they are occasionally disposed to force the hand of such writers; and, when
they succeed, their success may have deprived the
writers in question of a great part of their usefulness. If a Catholic writer of romance or fiction
writes only for a Catholic public there cannot be
too much Catholicity in his novels. But, if those
novels are to reach the public outside, there can
easily be too much: for they may be so vehemently
Catholic that the non-Catholic reader is frightened
away altogether. He says to himself: "The Catholic drum is being beaten too loud and insistently by
this novelist. I have had enough of him and shall
read him no more." That is hardly a point gained.
A great number of ears are lost, that might have
been gently educated, and an attention that might
have been attracted to the Church, her beauty, and
her truth, can no more be engaged by the writer in
question. Henceforth he may delight a Catholic
audience, and win its hearty applause, but what he
might have done, in drawing toward the faith them
who are without it, he has forfeited the chance of
doing. Yet it has not been his fault, but is the unfortunate result of having had his hand forced.

I think this does happen. A new writer appears
and there is something in his work that largely
attracts a public not given to the reading of Catholic
works: yet there is in his work that which marks it
Catholic. He is clearly on the Catholic side: there

seems a special sphere of service for him. Men are found reading him who never read a Catholic author before, and who listen with interest and attention to his quiet and reasonable presentment of Catholic ideas and things. He gives them a new conception of the sanity and wisdom of Catholic life and Catholic customs. What a good thing it would be, in such an instance, to leave well alone. But is it always left alone? That the writer is Catholic is plainly perceived by Catholics too: they cannot doubt it. They plainly recognize a clear hall-mark, and they too welcome the new writer in their fashion. But they cry loudly, "Here is a writer whom everybody reads, and a Catholic writer: why isn't he *more* Catholic?" In other words, why is he not undisguisedly controversial? Why are not his novels sermons on the Seven Sacraments, or the Celibacy of the Clergy, or the Doctrine of Purgatory? And if he do not very promptly conform to their ideals of a Catholic novelist, they may soon hint pretty loudly that he is not half a Catholic after all. The Catholics in his books, they begin to discover, are more like human beings than angels, and the non-Catholics are not monsters. He had there a fine opportunity of bringing in a conversion—and let it slip: and there he might have drawn a real saint—and didn't: and that scamp would very easily have been shown as a devil incarnate (without saying what he did), whereas he is no more than a scamp, and had some good points too, which scamps shouldn't have.

One result is that the Catholic writer, whom non-Catholics were listening to with some confidence, is listened to no longer by them. They perceive that something has happened to him. What has happened is that he has, being human, taken fright, and, in dread of being misunderstood by his own people, has succumbed to the least capable critics. He writes what they insist upon, but what those whom he might have gradually gained will not read at any price.

The perception of this sort of fact accounts, in my opinion, for the other fact that a considerable number of writers, who are really Catholics, and good ones too, are careful to write in such wise that their Catholicity does not appear at all. They choose a ground which appears to them safe: so long as they never go near the deeper interests of humanity they are on less contentious ground. No one will complain that a joke is not a Catholic joke; that a nursery-rhyme is void of Catholic intention; that a soliloquy by a tin soldier leaves out any allusion to the question of indulgences; that there is nothing truly Catholic about a dialogue between a Hippopotamus and a Chancellor of the Exchequer. Even a novel may escape censure which is merely pretty, or merely silly, or as shallow as a comic-opera. And they do pretty well. It doesn't matter a farthing to anybody whether they be Catholics or Confucians: they do not matter to anybody at all. Nobody asks whether the man inside the Punch-and-

Judy show is a Catholic, or the lady who leaps through paper hoops in a circus.

But ought we to scold them?

If it be assumed that they are, in fact, capable of better things: that there is a talent in a napkin: then we must feel regret that the napkin smothers it all. But part of the scolding is due to those indiscreet but excellent Catholics who have frightened them a little. We ought all to be heroic, but we are not all heroes: and it calls for a singular degree of courage to face the strict criticism of our own fellow-religionists who are, as I think, over-ready to demand of every Catholic foot that may appear that it should prove itself a whole Catholic Hercules —or get out.

But, if, on the other hand, there be no serious talent hidden away, and these good Catholic people, who are writing to make folk laugh, or make children merry, or keep alive for children the dear old realm of fairy-land (where nothing base is met, only the strange, the deliciously impossible, the lovely, and the gloriously happy), or even to amuse harmlessly the harmless necessary library-subscriber, then I think these writers are serving a good turn. They are occupying a ground that might else be occupied much amiss.

There will always be children, and, though most children may be nearer heaven than ourselves, they will not, commonly, be always thinking of it. And grown people are often babies: and some are not very wise: and some are silly enough: and many like to laugh—at indifferent jokes too: and library-subscribers will take out such novels, and are not every day in tune for books that *are* books in my sense of it; and young persons will hanker after tales about young persons much like themselves: and weddings and engagements will never be quite unpopular—nor denounced by our kindly Mother, the Church, either.

Is it best that all this matter should be produced by those who are not Catholics, who think the Church a folly or a nuisance, and religion an affectation or a bore, an anachronism or a fetter on the limbs of men and maidens? Should we be wise if we chased Catholic writers off this harmless ground, and left it open to occupation by people whose principles are all against the Church, whose sympathies are enlisted on the opposite side?

We *must* have a real Catholic press, and there are departments of literature which we *must* do all we can to make strongly, vigorously Catholic. The supply of Catholic, and deeply Catholic, writers, on theology, Scripture exegesis, hagiology, ecclesiastical and general history, sociology, and many other matters—including the *roman à thèse*—must be kept up. And, as we have already said, those who do their best to keep it up are rendering a special and vital service to religion.

But there *will* be the other sorts of writing and one of two things may happen in relation to them: either they may be abandoned to writers who are against the Church, and perhaps against all religion; or the ground may be largely occupied by writers who are Catholics, and who will slip in nothing adverse to faith or morals.

It seems to me quite possible to frighten Catholic writers off such ground altogether, or to cause them to feel that in occupying it they are falling into suspicion. That would be the case if they were made to feel that their fellow-Catholics held them to be failing to serve the good cause inasmuch as they were not doing more, doing something more definitely and undeniably on the Catholic side. Merely to frighten them off that harmless ground would be a great tactical error, and a great pity: because their gaps would be filled by people not harmless. But, as long as there is "a deal of human nature in a man" it would in all likelihood do worse harm; for the writing-man *must* write: it is part of his nature, as it is a part of other men's nature that they must be killing things. Nobody complains of a Catholic that he only shoots rabbits, though it would not matter at all to the Church if his rabbits were shot by an agnostic or a vehement Protestant. It would surely be a pity to scold away Catholics who feel they can write such matters as we have indicated because they are not writing something more obviously useful to religion. For the chances are they would go on writing and in worse company write, as it were, on the sly, keeping their faith up their sleeve, among folk who sympathized with *them* but were the reverse of sympathetic with the Church or religion of any color. I believe this does happen, and that where it happens, evil communications corrupt good manners, so that these originally harmless persons feel themselves in opposition, and pick up small antagonisms, because of the antagonism they have experienced.

If they were made to feel that in doing no more than writing harmlessly in harmless, if not exalted, departments of the press, fiction, and what not, they were doing good, though humble, service, it seems to me that it would be only just and would be wise.

Any square foot of territory occupied by a Catholic on good terms with his religion is a foot of ground lost to the occupation of the myriad forces arrayed against the Church in the press and in literature.

Is there sense in frowning down these good folk because they are only what they are?

Even in a monastery all are not abbots, or even choir-monks. But the lay-brother who cooks the dinner is a religious and is helping the cause of religion. Brother Porter may be a garrulous creature, and fond of a harmless exchange of news, and his daily talk with the butcher-boy, or the fishmonger, helps those persons to realize the humanism of monastic life. They do not, perhaps, see much of the abbot, or of Father Placid the great preacher: and those great men might not precisely know how to interest them. But Brother Porter does, and they acquire a rooted conviction that monasticism is not a dismal institution, nor an inhuman:

and it does them a little good. It did the Catholic
Church in England no disservice that for years
Punch was edited by a Catholic. He did not convert that organ into a weekly budget of controversy;
except that it was alive to the humors of Anglican
Episcopacy, it was not theological. But, with a
good Catholic in its editorial seat, there could be no
gibes at things sacred to us, no belittling of anything great in Catholic eyes: no light treatment of
matters we hold to be beyond the scope of laughter.
I do not say there is now—but there were times when
all the wit of *Punch* was pitted against the Pope.

Would it have been wisdom to insist that Sir
Francis Burnand should write only hagiology—or
else be skewered himself?

My impression is this: that many clean and decent, harmless, healthy novels, many inoffensive
plays, many wholesome tales for children, or for
boys, or big girls, are so because they were written
by undiscovered Catholics who feel in themselves no
aptitude for anything more clearly religious: if they
were frightened off, other books would be written,
by very different writers, neither clean, nor wholesome. Would that be a gain to religion?

Perhaps more encouragement would be more wise
toward these lay-brothers of letters.

It is not official discouragement that is depre-
cated: there is none. Those responsible for the
government of the Church, either in her headquar-
ters or elsewhere, are by no means addicted to interference. Nor does the discouragement come from

the clergy, but from a rather foolish class of lay persons, whom we have, in another place, endeavored to describe as the Weaker Brethren. It is one of their peculiarities to be unable to recognize the truth that God does not expect the majority of His creatures to do two things at once. Archbishops and bishops do not call upon Catholic lads playing cricket to demonstrate the Infallibility of the Church. If a Catholic writer wrote a funny skit on the Multiplication Table it would not be the clergy who complained that it did not, incidentally, confute the Three Chapters—that would be for an erudite Weaker Brother, the layman afflicted with a slight determination of Theology to the brain.

A pet accusation of outsiders against the Church is that of intolerance: an experience of five-and-thirty years teaches me that she is singularly tolerant and by no means addicted to fussy interference, that she is peculiarly disinclined to lend herself to "cranks," or frown on harmless people who may be doing a little good, in quite obscure fashion, because it is not a greater good and more striking in its methods. She is not given to quench flame that only smokes (your Weaker Brethren never smoke, they are above it); and she is not willing to call her lambs that skip, in a lambish manner, black little sheep. All that is the function of the Weaker Brethren, the bugbears of bishops, the skeletons in the good-natured cupboards of poor harassed, over-worked priests: the critics who never write anything or do anything themselves, but to whom there is a private, dismal, revelation how nothing should be done, and how everything should be written in some other fashion.

It is from the Weaker Brethren I would fain defend the Catholic writers who fill gaps that would else be filled by the Church's enemies, even though they fill them with nothing greater than a nursery-book, or a "smooth tale mostly of love," a poem something less than Shakespearean, or a comic effort that will be best relished by those whose idea of humor is not that of superior persons. If everybody only read the very best sort of book, or the most literary sort of newspaper, then nobody would have any business to produce middling books, or to help to produce popular papers. And they who, according to the measure of capacity God has given them, do try to add to the bulk of what is really literature, are helping religion in more ways than one. But they who are conscious of no such capacity, but are able to write as well, in their less literary sphere of operations, as their non-Catholic or anti-Catholic competitors, are they not, in helping to crowd out such competitors, but doing a service and deserving of some encouragement?

For my part I should be glad if all the comic papers (one need not read them) were written by Catholics, and all the funny plays, all the fairy-tales and nursery-books, all the novels that walk in hurried procession through the libraries and cannot walk too quick for me, and all the other stuff one sees people reading in trains and road-cars, which is certainly not literature, but might then be free of any graver fault.

The more Catholic encouragement such writers meet with the less likely are they really to need discouragement.

What the Weaker Brethren would insist upon is that all Catholics should be, like themselves, Superior Persons: whereas the Church only wants to lead us all to perfection, and that by many mean streets: for all decent people cannot inhabit the best quarters of the town. The Church's purview includes noisy places, and vulgar too: she has never proclaimed herself a monopoly of the genteel.

TWO DUTIES

A CERTAIN priest whose Sunday Mass was always served, and had for a number of years been served, by the same young man, on one occasion felt compelled to make him, on their return to the sacristy after Mass and sermon were over, a little apology. "On this Sunday last year I had," said he, "the same subject to preach about as to-day. It was a different sermon, but it had to deal with the same things; they are so bound up with the day, and so important. I am afraid, though, you and the congregation may have found the repetition rather tedious."

"Bless you, Father," the amiable creature replied cheerfully, "let's hope they weren't listening both times." Then, with a smile of engaging candor, "*I* wasn't."

The blessing, if irregular, was so cordially given that the priest accepted it gratefully, and the consolation too—as far as it went.

On this side of the Atlantic I have written on the Apostolate of the Press, and some things involved in it; but it is likely that no one on your side was listening. And that is why I would venture to take my parable again on the same theme with a different audience.

That Leo XIII and the late Sovereign Pontiff, Benedict XV have in very weighty words insisted on the necessity of Catholic journals the Catholic public is, in general, everywhere aware. Yet as George Eliot's Uncle Pullet "had a great natural faculty for ignorance," so some excellent people seem to have a surprising natural capacity for remaining ignorant of what their neighbours have long been talking about.

But as a whole the Catholic public is alive to the fact that two Popes have in recent years spoken strongly on the necessity of there being a powerful and efficient Catholic press. They quite perceive the necessity, and are all for a Catholic press equal in every way, and superior in some ways, to the huge non-Catholic press, which is alas! so often anti-Catholic.

What they do not, perhaps, seem to perceive so plainly is that an efficient Press must be flourishing, and that, in order that it may flourish, it must be vigorously supported. One necessity of a strong and effectual Catholic Press they do understand—that able and willing Catholic writers should be forthcoming. They *are* forthcoming both in England and in America: and, on both sides of the Atlantic, they are willing as well: willing to forego the chances of much higher pay for their work than would be theirs if their services were not mainly reserved for Catholic journals and a Catholic audience. In thus reserving their services Catholic writers exercise another sort of self-denial, and a higher: for every writer naturally prefers the widest audience possible: the wider the audience the greater natural stimulus is there to a writer. Just as empty benches naturally chill a preacher, and a packed church warms him as well as it, so is it with a writer. And this is not merely because of the greater chance of applause but because of the wider hope of sympathy and understanding. Nevertheless, both on this side of the Atlantic and yours, I repeat that Catholic writers show themselves perfectly ready to devote themselves to the service of the Catholic Press, regardless of smaller pecuniary rewards, and of a smaller audience.

But, whether the Catholic public is equally loyal in support is another question. In England I doubt if it is. How it may be in America, I do not know for certain.

This at all events is certain: that the Apostolate of the Press depends not on the Press itself alone. However authoritative the mission of an apostle may be, however unsparing of himself he may be, however noble his message, and competent his presentation of it—he must have hearers. And if people will not listen he cannot have them.

And more: even an apostolate as that of Apostles or apostolic men to unbelieving nations, implies certain material things, a certain equipment. But such an apostolate as that of the Press demands an equipment that is extremely costly. In this case zeal and self-sacrifice alone is not enough. To carry on an able and efficient Press campaign implies great expense and a Catholic Press must be crippled, and ultimately silenced, unless it is maintained by an adequate and efficient response to meet that expense.

Catholics are not always backward in criticism of their own Press: they expect it to equal the general Press in literary power and in appearance too. The paper must not be flimsy; the type must not be unsightly; the illustrations must be first-rate; the news of the newest, the reviews striking and original, and the editorship in fact of the highest degree of excellence. Well, all this costs money. And the money can only be available if the Catholic Press be as well supported as the Press which is not Catholic. And that support must mainly, and in the first instance, be given by Catholics themselves.

A Catholic paper may do worlds of good by coming into non-Catholic hands. But it cannot if it does not exist, and its existence must be contingent on the coöperation of the Catholic Public.

All this may seem a mere string of truisms. But some truisms are largely ignored—as that, if you spend more than comes in to you, you will end in debt and disaster. If then the Catholic Press is not to end in debt and disaster, as much must come into it as it pays out to make itself and keep itself what the Catholic Public expects it to be: and what comes in must come from the Catholic public chiefly. Does every Catholic family regularly subscribe to even one Catholic paper? Few are the families, even among the quite poor people in which one, and

often more than one, non-Catholic paper is not regularly taken. Some of these non-Catholic papers
are good enough: some are bad enough: and many
are silly, worthless, and such as to require an antidote. Almost all, it is seriously to be borne in mind
by Catholics, are written by people who have no religious beliefs at all, or whose religious beliefs, such
as they are, are wholly alien from our own, often
very inimical, often supercilious and scornful of
every Catholic ideal, often permeated by thoroughly lax morality—as for instance in regard to
the sanctity and indissolubility of Christian marriage. Even comic papers, which would seem to be
neutral ground, sin very heavily in this respect: the
whole point (what there is of it) of half the jokes in
many of them presupposes that marriage itself is a
joke, though a bad one: that conjugal infidelity is
another joke, and a better one. And it is largely
assumed by them that religion is a bore, a convention, and a pretence: that straightforward folk discard the nuisance and the false pretence.

The presence of such papers in Catholic households needs at least an antidote; and Catholic papers are the obvious and indispensable antidote.

The public atmosphere of life in almost all "civil-
ized" countries is not only un-Catholic but irreligious. At best it mostly assumes that religion has
nothing to do or say with public life: that, if a man
chooses to be religious it is a personal idiosyncrasy,
and he must do it at his own cost, and keep it quiet.
Anti-Christ may make all the noise he can, but Chris-

tianity is a private fad and is not to annoy the public.

And, meanwhile, it is in this atmosphere that Catholics are to live and breathe. In the hygiene of the body men are growing more and more alert to the necessity of precaution and antidote. Where circumstances imply risk, measures of self-defence are adopted: those who are forced to encounter vitiated air are warned how to minimize danger of infection. But is the breathing of an atmosphere inimical to Christian faith and morality less hazardous? If inevitable, are we excused from arming ourselves with such antidotes and safeguards as lie in our power?

Catholics in business, in society, and at play, are everywhere exposed to an infective atmosphere. It is breathed around them by the public Press, and by the daily discussion of every topic they hear spoken of. Many who create it they perceive, or believe, to be clever, intelligent, capable people—more so, perhaps, than themselves. Scientists will tell us in alarming figures the weight of the physical atmosphere upon our heads: who can measure the weight of this un-Christian atmosphere upon the heads, hearts, and morals of our Christian people?

There are supernatural antidotes: we do not forget them. God's grace and His sacraments are still with us. But the reason we do not now speak of them here is that many of those subjected to the influences we mention do not in fact make use of those supernatural safeguards against them. Catholic newspapers are not to supersede the Church's sacraments, but to help powerfully in bringing the memory of them and of all other means of grace to the minds of her children.

I should like to say a word as to what may be called Catholic insulation.

The circumstances of modern life do largely insulate from Catholic surroundings, Catholic ideals, and even Catholic memories, large numbers of our people. Even families feel it: there are places where this or that Catholic family finds itself, or imagines itself, to be so placed as to be without Catholic society of its own calibre. Social inequalities exist even in republics: perhaps nowhere more than in republics are such inequalities more insisted upon. Where there are no titles, and where theoretically there is no rank, other distinctions are all the more perceived by those that have them. Many families in a republican state are well-born, and they do not forget it: others are intellectual, well-educated, cultured, refined. Where there are not families of corresponding birth, breeding, or mental superiority they miss it, and are not inclined to merge their own real or supposed advantages altogether. A Catholic family with such claims to superiority in a restricted neighbourhood where other Catholic families of their own sort are few or absent, will probably mix largely if not entirely in non-Catholic circles: and as long as human nature is what it is this will be so. This is one sort of Catholic insulation.

Then there is the much commoner case of individual Catholics, separated from home and family:

young men and young women who have gone out
into the world to earn their bread. They often
live, and sometimes are almost bound to live, among
people who have not their faith, or who have no
faith of any kind. These people among whom their
lives are lived may be bad and repulsive, or bad and
by no means repellent, or "good" in a way that is
not the Church's way; at any rate their influence is
not on the Church's side. This is another sort of
Catholic insulation.

In both the insulated Catholic family or individual is subject to the continual erosion of forces
stronger and more persistent than could easily be
exaggerated. There is a more than daily influx of
a tide that would be irresistible but for omnipotent
grace.

The counter-influence, against such erosion,
against the diurnal tides of doubt and chill, which
might be effected by the constant use of Catholic
papers is really enormous.

Such insulation tends to make Catholic households and Catholic individuals wholly forgetful of
what the Church is, what her work is, what are her
struggles at home and abroad, her interests, her
preoccupations, her daily martyrdom, her noble energies, her self-sacrifice, her vital power, her undying and undiminished importance, her intellectual
superiority, her moral preëminence, her Divine authority, and her unabated claims. Catholics thus
isolated are by the use of Catholic papers put in in-

evitable and indespensable reminder of these the forgotten things.

The insulation we speak of tends directly to a sort of selfishness and meanness of outlook. A nobler spirit of community and fellowship is directly engendered and fostered by reading of what the world-wide energies of the Church are. The habitual use of Catholic papers forbids a Catholic to assume that his Church is obsolete or behind-hand. It compels him to ask himself whether it be not he who is a sluggard and *faineant*. It whets his zeal, and stimulates his sympathy: it begets brotherly love and an emulation in good.

In the United States there are published immense numbers of Catholic journals, magazines, reviews, and what not, in English, German, French, Italian, and Spanish. They are not cutting each other's throats: there is not one too many. If some might be better than they are, can they be made better without more efficient support? If many are as good as they could conceivably be, would not their efficiency be immensely increased if the number of their readers were what it might easily be?

The efficiency of a paper, or a review, does not depend merely on its own excellence: the noblest preacher that ever stood in a pulpit would preach in vain if nobody stopped to listen. And no matter how good the Catholic Press may be, its apostolate can only bear fruit among those whom it reaches.

We end, therefore, with the question with which

we set out—Is the Catholic Press adequately supported by the Catholic Public? If not, is our duty done when an adequate Catholic Press is provided? If we wish to carry out the papal mandate, we have not only to supply the Catholic papers but to do all in our power to foster and enlarge the demand on which the supply must in the long run depend.

THE END